Praise fo

This is a companion to keep by your side to bring peace, order and exploration to this thing we call life that has so many moving parts that can become jumbled. Karrie provides clear choices for strategies and steps one can take which are reflected through the stories of Nadia, Camryn, Harper and Jade. You will find yourself in this book whether you're dealing with self-care, dealing with clutter, regaining equilibrium with your friends, what moves you, parenting and more. From the practical to the personal, Karrie simplifies life's challenges everyone hits at some point and shows you a way through to live your best life starting today. If not now, when?

~ *Karla Robertson*
CEO Shifting Gears® - Mental Agility Coaching

From the moment I met Karrie, I knew she was another mentoring mom who was put in this world to help other women navigate life in business and motherhood. Helping women preserve their precious family memories and sharing solid and personalized solutions for the challenges so many of us face is truly a gift. Taking the time to read her book is the self-care you deserve and it's filled with fabulous ideas to help you!

~ *Sherra Humphreys*
Owner, Simple Photo Stories & Mother of Four

Girlfriend Stories provides an innovative and compassionate perspective for addressing challenges that we all face in our daily lives. None of us are carbon copies of each other, so why are we constantly searching for the one "right" way to navigate the difficult situations we face day-to-day? I love how Girlfriend Stories reminds us all to tap into our innate strengths and wisdom to find solutions, and also lean on support when we need it.

~ *Heather Doyle Fraser*
Publisher. Author. Coach.
Compassionate Mind Collaborative

You'll see yourself in the archetypes in Girlfriend Stories.

Girlfriend Stories invites you into the challenges faced by the modern woman and her family while providing tips about how to approach these challenges through the lens of different personality types. You'll discover simple and invaluable tips for solving the myriad of challenges the modern family faces from de-cluttering the family home, packing for vacation, laundry duty, administrative organization, and my personal favorite, "Family Device Management." I wish I would have had this chapter when I was raising my family.

~ *Dana Frost*
Vitally You® podcast host, Master Life Coach,
Functional Nutrition and Lifestyle Practitioner

Girlfriend Stories

Girlfriend Stories

an individualized approach
to create more time
& solve everyday challenges

Karrie Converse-Jones

TurningLeaf Enterprises Publishing

Published 2022

Book Design: Karrie Converse-Jones
Book Layout: accuracy4sure@gmail.com
Copyeditor: Ashley Scoby
Cover Design: Diane Lorenzo
Editor: Heather Doyle Fraser
Illustrator: Morgan Jones
Marketing: Jesse Sussman
Proofer: Julie Homon

Printed in the United States of America

ISBN - 979-8-9861674-0-4 (Paperback)
ISBN - 979-8-9861674-1-1 (eBook)

First Edition

TurningLeaf Enterprises Publishing - Westerville, Ohio

To the family that supports
every one of my ideas.
I don't have the words to express my love.

Contents

Part 1

Getting to Know Your Girlfriend

Why this Book?

I'm never one to shy away from learning a tip or trick to make life easier. However, sometimes advice doesn't seem to "fit" for me. Either it ran opposite to who I am and how I live, or it seemed overwhelming. If I personally developed an approach and shared it with girlfriends, I found the same problem—for some, the tip would work, but for others, it seemed foreign. I began to think about the diversity of women who could benefit from sharing ideas, and how to share them in a way that would actually work for them.

Who are these girlfriends in our lives?

The women with whom I have shared ideas or suggestions are usually professionals (inside or outside the home) from thirty-five to fifty-five years old. They are lifelong learners and curious about various topics. These women—as mothers, aunts, sisters, or young grandparents—have children in their lives in some form.

For these girlfriends, time is the ultimate luxury, and they work hard to carve as much time out of their twenty-four-hour days as possible. They are action-oriented and heart-centered doers, who care about everyone in their lives, but struggle to prioritize themselves equally.

Why this approach?

I've worked hard to identify who I am and what I offer the world. I have come to realize that my purpose is:

Sharing information as a service that inspires action and connection through experiences.

By connecting with others and sharing experiences, we can learn more about solutions to life's challenges. However, in this sharing, it is evident that women may tackle the same challenges differently because of their strengths and tendencies.

Self-help information assumes everyone can use the same approach to achieve the same results. Then, when we can't seem to put into practice what we have learned, there is that sense of failure, and we go searching for the next self-help nugget that might be a better fit.

Challenges are common, but getting to the same end is a different journey for each person. Tailoring the steps and expectations to who you are helps create confidence that you can make changes and achieve success. I want to inspire any girlfriend to accomplish what they want in the way that works for them.

What is the Approach?

The internet has allowed our curious minds to take various assessments and quizzes to learn more about ourselves. Often these types of assessments are given in the workplace as part of team-building activities. You may recognize some of these common assessments and your results in the table.

If you have not taken any of these assessments before, see the links at the end of the chapter to pause and take one (or more!). There is no preference, but you will need the results of at least one to move forward in this book.

Has it been a while since you took one of these? It is worth re-taking, as some of our traits change over time, while others are core to who we are.

As you determine your assessment results which are loosely grouped together across assessments, you will identify with a girlfriend or two listed at the top of the columns.

Who are the girlfriends in this book?

These girlfriends are broad portraits of each assessment type, so you can see yourself in their shoes. You may find that you relate to more than one type. That's not a problem! You may also identify with another role's tendencies.

Assessments	***Camryn***	***Jade***	***Harper***	***Nadia***
16 Personalities	***Analysts***	***Diplomats***	***Sentinels***	***Explorers***
	architects	advocates	logistican	virtuosos
	logicians	mediators	defenders	adventurers
	commanders	protagonists	executives	entrepre-neurs
	debaters	campaigners	consuls	entertainers
Clifton Strengths*	***Influencing***	***Relationship Building***	***Strategic Thinking***	***Executing***
Keirsey	***Rational***	***Idealist***	***Guardian***	***Artesian***
	field marshal	teacher	supervisor	composer
	inventor	champion	provider	crafter
	mastermind	counselor	protector	performer
	architect	healer	inspector	promoter
Meyers-Briggs	INTJ architect	INFJ advocate	ISTJ inspector	ISTP crafter
	INTP thinker	INFP mediator	ISFJ protector	ISFP artist
	ENTJ commander	ENFJ giver	ESTJ director	ESTP persuader
	ENTP debater	ENFP champion	ESFJ care-giver	ESFP performer

*Formerly Strengths Finder

Every chapter in the book presents a challenge, and details of how each girlfriend tackled it based on who they are. Feel free to review the stories and steps for one or all of these girlfriends. You may also recognize a close friend, partner, spouse, or sibling in another girlfriend.

For links to these assessments, please visit:
www.girlfriendstoriesbook.com

Free Results

16Personalities: *Personality Types*
Keirsey: *Temperaments*

Paid or Professional Partner Needed

CliftonStrengths: *Unique Strengths*
Meyers-Briggs: *How Someone Thinks*

Who Am I In This Book?

Have you found your girlfriend? Are you ready to get to know her a bit more?

Just like when you and three of your girlfriends gather for coffee (or drinks!), you may notice that you relate to one or more of these women and see yourself living a similar lifestyle or responding to situations in similar ways. Ideally, there is one girlfriend you most identify with and can see yourself tackling a challenge in the same way—which can set your expectations of success. Instead of a cookie-cutter answer of how to approach a challenge, you can follow the steps that make sense specifically to you and your girlfriend!

To establish that relationship and help you get to know these girlfriends a little more intimately, their stories are here at the beginning.

Camryn

Hey there, I'm Camryn. I'm a single mom of two great girls: one in sixth and one in eighth grade. I live in a big city in what we call a "cozy" apartment (read: somewhat small!).

I have a great job and have rapidly worked my way up the corporate ladder. It's demanding, but I've earned a lot of flexibility, which is great since I always seem to be looking for more time (between juggling work and the girls' activities).

I try to set a good example for my girls. We have a close relationship, and I've raised them to focus on experiences more than things. I want them to grow up aware of the broader world and the problems people face.

I'm a planner and am someone who relies on my knowledge coupled with my intuition. Whether dealing with a leader at the office or a relationship that is not a good fit, I can innately tell when something is wrong. I can look back and pinpoint the times where my internal voice was saying something was out of balance, and I felt out of alignment with a situation or friendship. It took me many years to realize that I physically feel in my body when a situation or decision is not suitable for me. Now, by paying attention to these signals, I can quickly return to a balanced state.

When I set my mind to something, I go after it, whatever it is. I often sound like I have an answer for everything (even when I don't). Couple this with my sarcastic streak, and I'm aware people perceive me as intimidating. I wish they didn't, as it's not my intention.

I also have a great imagination and am a hotbed of new ideas. I love getting an idea or project started, but when it reaches a certain level of detail, I know I need to look to others who are great at handling those specifics. It's not that I cannot focus: I will pay attention and work hard to see things through. But I can lose interest when something becomes routine.

My circle of friends is pretty small. Between work and kids, I don't factor in much time to enhance and nurture these relationships. I feel like I can be a fiercely loyal friend, but it may not be evident because I'm not devoting time. Maybe I'm not a good friend?

I have one brother and one sister, but both live elsewhere. I am afraid of going through life without these close connections, so I'd like to deepen and expand my circle. But I know I will need to bring more attention to my relationships to accomplish this.

Jade

Hello, my name is Jade. I'm a forty-four-year-old mom of two. I've been married for just over nineteen years to an old soul I have known for a long time. My kids are working their way through the high school experience: My son is a junior, and my daughter just started as a freshman at the same high school.

I believe I am here to make the world a better place. That is the who and the why. I struggle with the what, where, and how in my life. I know this seems a bit lofty, and I worry about how people perceive me. I can't fake who I am, but it's hard to find the tribe that understands me.

I involve myself in several volunteer activities, which are fulfilling. I don't lead; I just quietly contribute and have that feed my spirit. I know I'm a bit of a dreamer who doesn't seem to fit into this volatile world. I'm sure people think I'm flaky, but I have always envisioned working towards a higher purpose for myself.

I also live in my imagination, so much so that I sometimes think I've accomplished more than I have. It's a bit of a letdown. I view success differently, I guess. I fantasize about things I still want to do, especially travel. I tack up pictures in my home office to keep those dreams on the horizon. But I don't make specific plans to get there.

The truth is, it seems I always need to go run an errand or take care of something I forgot. It's hard for me to keep a list of all the tasks at hand. What's worse is I'm afraid some of this has rubbed off on my kids. My son is a bit introverted and a video gamer. I think he enjoys fantasy more than real life and struggles with completing his daily school assignments. My daughter is an artist and seems to work well in every medium she tries. It's like the creativity simply flows from her. However, this means she will avoid anything that isn't art, which doesn't always align academically. I know they are both smart, but they are a bit outside the mainstream of high school. Still, they are empathetic and kind, which makes me proud.

My parents have passed, but I do have family that gathers together regularly and is inclusive of my kids. My sisters and their families are involved in our major events, and we do the same with their families. There is a wide variety of ages in all of our children, and I'm careful to let my kids develop their own relationships with their cousins to hopefully create lasting friendships.

For myself, I search for practices that can sustain positive energy in my life. Right now, I am slowly mastering a regular yoga practice. In a good week, I am on my mat for an hour; however, most weeks I am lucky to practice twice for a quick fifteen minutes. I wish I could build in more structure to get everything I want to get done, or maybe go wherever I want to go!

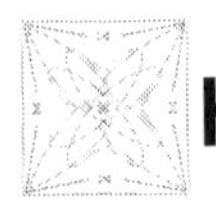

Harper

Hi, nice to meet you. My name is Harper. I am thirty-seven, married, and we live outside the suburbs on a large piece of land. I don't work outside the home because I take care of everything for my family, including our three children: my daughter in elementary school and my two sons in middle school.

I am a serious planner, and I keep many calendars to track everything. I love to-do lists, and I keep extensive ones to check off. I like to do all this on paper, which I know can be annoying. I'm not that into technology beyond using my smartphone for phone calling, texting, photos, and GPS. I enjoy being outside, and often on the weekends, we are all working around our property, which is more important to me than my device.

I want to make life picture-perfect wherever I can. I also like to be efficient. With any task from vacuuming to carpooling, I'm trying to think of ways to improve it, so I love thinking of even more ideas. This is probably why I also single-handedly host most of our family gatherings—that way, things get done right so everyone can enjoy themselves.

I have a small group of mom friends, and I am the leader of several local groups, including PTO, a charity in our town, and a church group for women. But I do not like to get involved in other people's drama, and I dislike gossip. We are in our groups for a reason, and we need to stay focused. Everyone in the groups I lead understands we don't have time for that extra stuff.

I am a caregiver to my parents. They are in an assisted living facility, but I am constantly worried about their health and safety. I visit them often to bring groceries, cook meals to freeze, and take care of their house. This is a recent turn of events and a bit of an internal struggle for me. I feel like now I'm the parent, and they are the children, but that's not right. I don't always know how to interact with them as this dynamic shifts. It's added an extra layer of activity to my life, and I wonder if I'm becoming buried in the layers.

Nadia

I'm Nadia. Good to meet you. I'm thirty-three years old and have been married to my wife for almost eight years. We met in college, so we've been together even longer. I have a part-time job, while my wife is the primary income provider. We have two children: a twenty-eight-month-old son and a daughter in first grade. We are still in our first home in an old neighborhood, so moving up to a larger home is our next challenge.

I feel a bit agitated lately, as everything seems to be falling into a routine. I know that is important to kids, but it is so dull. Am I failing as a mom by not planning out everything? It's hard to randomly try something new or fun on the weekends when it seems like the kids' schedules take over everything (from activities to naps). I wish I was more of a structured person, but it's just not that interesting to me. I'm trying to think of ways to make these boring, routine activities as simple as possible so I don't have to be invested in them: Do it, and it's done!

At least the kids bring a sense of wonder to my life. Seeing things from their child-like perspective makes me feel like I'm seeing things for the first time, which expands my appreciation of their curiosity.

Honestly, I feel like I'm settling: that married life and kids leave no room to be impulsive or even to be me, for that matter. I constantly feel a sense of inner turmoil and conflict because I don't feel I'm being true to myself. I love my wife and children and would do anything for them, but day-to-day life can be mundane. I then lose focus on the ordinary, which makes me appear scattered and unorganized. Maybe I am.

I feel a sense of restlessness. Where is the newness or excitement in my days? If I tackle some things on my never-ending to-do list, can I somehow make this to-do thing interesting? I can try approaching a project as something new to explore and try. Maybe that will help. But am I manufacturing excitement? Is that good enough to get me through?

It boils down to seeking passion in all things. Passion then feeds energy, which feeds excitement. I don't want to spend my days without that. It's like wasting the time I have been granted in life. I already feel like I will look back with some level of regret, which I don't want as a burden.

How Do I Use This Book?

There is a framework to using this book. Now that you have your girlfriend identified, tracking her journey throughout the book will help you understand what next steps you can take to tackle the challenges.

The three parts of this book help you develop externally and internally. You can generate change for yourself, and then expand that change to impact others.

Part 1
Getting to Know Your Girlfriend

You are here. This is where you assess and identify your corresponding girlfriend(s). Knowing these friends can help you track the recommendations that follow every challenge. As you move through the book, you have several options:

Read straight through - If you are a book-lover, you probably can't help it and will get to know all the girlfriends!

Hop around by challenge - Take a look at the challenge and see whether it's something you are interested in. If not, feel free to move on!

Follow your girlfriend. Read in whichever order you prefer, but only read the next steps your particular friend takes!

Part 2
Your Girlfriend's Guide to Improving Places and Things

This part focuses on day-to-day challenges and how to simplify them. The content is focused on individual transformation—changes you can make that maybe no one but you will notice. Later chapters have challenges that may impact how your family operates, and you may need their buy-in to make these changes. However, they will make a difference in the time and effort you spend on these activities in your life.

Part 3
Your Girlfriend's Guide to Growing with Family and Friends

These chapters focus more on actions you can take to possibly change or improve your relationships. Again, these challenges may be internal or personal first, then expand to encompass family and other meaningful relationships.

In Parts 2 and 3, you will also find two bonus chapters focused on self-care. Each girlfriend tries a form of self-care that may push them out of their comfort zone, but can bring some much-needed healing energy.

Structure

To breakdown the structure of each chapter, you will find:

The Challenge

A clear statement of what challenge this chapter tackles.

The Story

A personal story from one of our four girlfriends describing how a particular challenge impacts her daily life and the concerns she struggles with.

Taking Action

Information to help you move forward in tackling this challenge.

Ways to Get Started

Recommended next steps based on your girlfriend's personality type. Some types may tackle the challenge head-on; others may take baby steps. Regardless of the approach, these suggestions will set you up for success. The best part? There is no failure, as any step forward (in alignment with who you are) is progress.

Takeaway

This is a closing summary of the action and provides you with the opportunity to take note of how you want to commit to tackling this challenge.

What's one small step you can take today?

A space to jot down or doodle what actions you want to take, large or small.

Stories paired with step-by-step instruction creates two powerful ways to ingrain something new. The combination of both in this book, coupled with the journeys of your girlfriends, can lead to your success in driving personal change.

For more information on products and services noted in these chapters, please see: www.girlfriendstoriesbook.com

Part 2

Your Girlfriend's Guide to Improving Places and Things

1

Quick Room Refresh

The Challenge

My home feels dreary—boring even. I'm not finding joy or sanctuary in my rooms, just the feeling there is too much stuff and not enough inspiration.

Camryn's Story

As the winter months approach, I'm restless about our apartment space. I think it's a nice-sized apartment for us, but now I feel like we are packed to the gills. It seems like every room is full. There are things piling up in all the closets and cabinets, and the drawers are crammed with items I'm not sure we even need.

Plus, when I look over each room, there is no sense of my style. When I was married and had a house, I knew I had a good eye for coordinating color, shape, and space, but it is not apparent here. Why have I ignored these spaces?

I don't have a lot of room in my budget for home decor. I am not a shopper, and I don't like to buy an item if it doesn't have some greater personal meaning. I'm disappointed my space isn't more uplifting. My girls decorated their rooms with such energy and liveliness. What does it say I haven't bothered with the rest of my home?

Taking Action

A great way to fight through the clutter is by taking little steps. Tackling a bit at a time allows you to edit your items without the overwhelming feeling of tackling the entire home. Working through the house and feeling that weight of stuff lifted, you may see possibilities to refresh rooms you didn't see before.

One Drawer at a Time

When thinking about organizing or reducing clutter across the home, the idea can be daunting. Instead of tackling it all, emptying one drawer or clearing one shelf in every room in the house can be part of the regular house-cleaning routine.

- Dresser in the master bedroom? Clear the bottom drawer, so it is empty.

- Entertainment center in the living room? Clear one drawer (or cabinet, or shelf), so it is empty.

- Linen closet: one shelf empty.

- Kitchen: make one shelf in a cabinet empty!

Why? Having one drawer or small cabinet empty can provide the feeling of breathing room. The house isn't "packed to the gills" with stuff no one remembers owning and items not being utilized. By tackling just one spot, you can ask, "Does this truly belong? Do I utilize or value it? Is it in the right spot?" Answers to these questions can quickly help you see whether or not you want it, then determine where it actually belongs.

It doesn't mean the shelf or drawer stays empty forever. But leaving it bare for a while might feel as good as spreading out the remaining items to other locations.

Quick Room Refresh

While clearing drawers or shelves, you might find some hidden treasures you forgot all about. Use these to inspire a quick room refresh. Like the home decorating shows suggest, go around the house and pull together items that inspire, but may be scattered. Whether they're items purchased on vacations, gifts, or personal inspirational pieces, walking around the house "hunting" for these treasures hiding in plain sight can be interesting.

Think about items that lend themselves to a theme or style:

- A "beachy" look with shells and wood furniture.

- An "art gallery" showcasing multiple pieces of children's artwork hung museum-style.

- Accessories of a similar color grouped to provide visual variety in an area.

- A "sanctuary" of sorts with most of the candles and plants gathered in one spot.

- A "hall of fame" with all sports memorabilia and souvenirs defining one room.

Pulling similar items—both furniture and accessories—into one area can define a look for a room.

Meanwhile, clearing out one empty drawer in every room can provide both physical and mental space. When you have that space, perhaps you'll become more open and eager to freshen things up.

Ways to Get Started

Clearing clutter and bringing deliberate focus to an area of your home can breathe new life to a neglected space.

Camryn

Camryn has an under-utilized corner of the family room, since it's not across from the television. She has some spare chairs and a small table there, with a few large books on the floor behind it. Camryn looks around the apartment and starts thinking about creating a "reading nook." To do this she:

- Drags out a larger table from another room and removes the little table.

- Moves an unused floor lamp from another corner of the room to behind the chairs.

- Gathers up travel-themed coffee table books from various trips, along with her favorite bookends.

- Pulls together some framed family vacation photos to decorate the tabletop.
- Digs up a large basket from her bedroom and fills it with multiple blankets and throws the girls typically only use in the winter.
- Pulls from the hall closet some throw pillows she thought she no longer needed.

Within minutes she has a stylish and welcoming reading nook, just next to the fireplace. This activity inspires Camryn to look critically at spots in other rooms to brainstorm what she could "shop" for in her own home. Pulling those items together, she can infuse her style into the space, without ever going to the store.

 Jade

Jade feels like she is always fighting clutter. She also thinks she is the primary cause of the chaos, thanks to her impulse purchases. Jade decides she needs input from the rest of the family to help reduce clutter.

Jade starts tackling one storage area at a time in a room—a dresser, a desk, the entertainment cabinet, it doesn't matter. She pulls everything out and sorts to determine what she keeps and what she still questions. Then she brings in her kids, points to the unsure pile, and asks, "If you moved out tomorrow, would you take this with you?"

At first, the kids think this is crazy. How would they know what they would need? But most of these items are non-essential, so the kids aren't interested in the bulk of what Jade shows them. With that secondary validation, Jade feels confident in pulling together everything unnecessary and donating it somewhere it can actually be used.

Harper

Looking around the house, Harper never feels her family has a lot of clutter. She keeps tight control over how many unnecessary things are bought. Still, after living for so long in one home, she knows she cannot help but accumulate stuff. Harper likes the idea of clearing out things even where they are not in plain sight. Every Saturday while the family completes chores, she tackles a drawer—just one, so it doesn't take long.

First, she simply reduces—looking for anything unnecessary, unused, or inexpensive enough to quickly replace. She keeps her focus on one room every week until she's gone through every drawer, cabinet, and shelf.

Once she thoroughly examines the room, she returns to see if she can reach the goal of one empty drawer. Harper looks through all drawers for potential consolidation, and uses a stack of organizers to help keep order. With less stuff, it is much easier to rearrange a bit and leave one drawer empty. Harper has a true sense of satisfaction that her rooms are becoming clutter-free, even in the places you can't see.

Nadia

Nadia knows the kids' toys are taking over. Every room has so much that she is constantly pushing it all into a corner. Did these things multiply at night? Usually, she is laid back when it comes to this mess. So if it's getting to her, she knows it must be out of control.

One evening once the kids are in bed, she and her wife pull all the toys from one room together. They keep the things the kids are most interested in playing with and toss the rest into a laundry basket they then tuck away in a closet. The next night they do the same and continue until they are through all the first-floor rooms. Next, they pull out the (now) four laundry baskets and go through the "toy rubble," as Nadia calls it. They look for pieces that make a toy whole again and determine if the kids will still enjoy it. Any toy no longer needed goes into a box for donation.

They wait until a Friday night, then decide to turn their unused formal living room into a dedicated playroom. They remove some unused furniture and tables and put them in the garage to try to sell locally online. They bring in some large pillows, various boxes and tubs for storage, and, of course, the remaining toys from around the house. Nadia even prints out pictures of the kids' favorite characters and hangs them around the room.

The next morning is like Christmas to their children—it's funny to see them race through the room like every toy is new. The kids play in the room most of the day while Nadia and her wife relax in their toy-free family room. Nadia isn't sure how long the clear family room will last, but in her mind, knowing everything will return to one room at the end of the day is a success.

Takeaway

It takes effort to create inspiring spaces in the home. Sometimes it is actually the mental clutter we are trying to clear when we tackle the physical clutter. If clutter of any kind is overwhelming, start by emptying or clearing small bits of space in a room. This can reinforce your need for space and openness in other aspects of your life—which can kick off your journey to continue this expansion and improvement.

What's one small step you can take today?

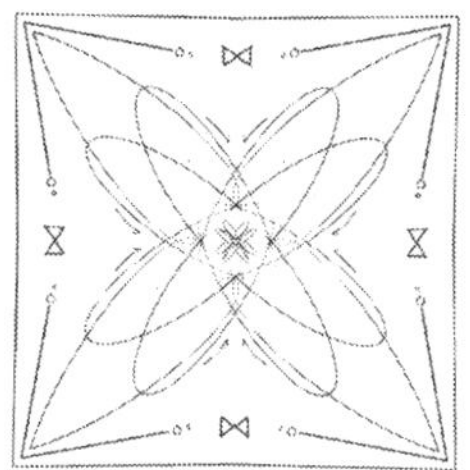

2

Digital Photo Overwhelm

The Challenge

When I think of my family photos, all I can think of is a digital mess somewhere between my computer and phone. These are precious memories captured for both posterity and enjoyment—but I'm not enjoying them. Now I receive messages that my phone is full and I don't know what to do.

Harper's Story

I can't find my photos. I am uncomfortable with that statement because I am organized in many ways, but my digital photos are a game of whack-a-mole. The photos pop up on my phone, then on my computer. I delete them from one place, and they show up again on another device.

I know they are in a "cloud," but I don't understand how that helps me access or enjoy them. It seems like the number of photos are increasing, as we all take so many, but are they worth keeping? I personally take many photos of magazine articles, receipts, and screenshots of inspirational quotes, but I don't need to keep them in my library of photos. I need to pull everything together before I lose track of my photos.

Taking Action

There are some questions to ask yourself when thinking about organizing a digital collection of family photos:

If my photos were all organized, what would I do with them? How could my family enjoy them?

- Frame memorable images to display?
- Send digital copies to the family?
- Make printed photo books of the best ones?
- Watch a slideshow on the TV or computer?

Once you have this vision, determine if there is a year, topic, or event meaningful for you:

- All your son's soccer photos in one book showcasing his efforts from elementary school to high school.

- A beautiful digital slideshow of your fabulous vacation set to music.

- The last five years of family group photos hung on your wall.

Start small and pull only the photos that fit one of your goals off your physical devices. This involves pulling together phones, old digital cameras, thumb drives, SD cards, and even email attachments.

You also need to consider any backup cloud storage solutions you have in place. Depending on the type of cloud storage, you may be limited on how many photos you can download and work with. In addition, for the photos stored in the cloud, note the date stamps. This detail can go missing when the photo reaches your hard drive.

Video files are often integrated with photo files. Think about what video files mean to you, and again, how you would want to enjoy them. Do you want to store them with the photos, so everything from one event is captured together? Or do you want to pull the videos into one place to navigate through? Do you have the storage capacity to do both?

Afraid of getting sidetracked by other images? See if a child or friend can help, and make it into a game. For example, ask them to find every photo with a soccer uniform or soccer ball in it.

Ways to Get Started

Whether it's to gain more space, remove duplicate files, or preserve family memories, tackling those photo files can provide peace of mind.

Camryn

Camryn loves capturing and enjoying family photos, but at this point, her daughters take a lot more pictures on their phones than she does. Unfortunately, she never sees these photos, since they live on her daughters' devices. She worries that photos from trips and events will be lost due to a damaged cell phone one day.

What's worse, Camryn takes pictures of things she feels she needs to temporarily document, including travel receipts, texts from friends, even pictures of items in stores. It seems that capturing photos means she doesn't have to work hard to remember something, but these are brief references and nothing she needs to keep forever.

Camryn doesn't think she has the room for all these photos on her home computer, and she won't put them on her work laptop. From previous research, Camryn believes an external hard drive will be the perfect solution. Once she has an external drive hooked to her home computer, she creates a folder for each phone and uploads the photos she doesn't want to lose forever.

When copying the photos to the hard drive, she realizes how much room these photos take up. Once she is done copying, she deletes all previous years' pictures on every phone; only the current year remains. Their phones suddenly have tons of space again!

Then, she asks each of her daughters to go through the folder on the hard drive and sort all photos and videos into two folders: personal and family. The family ones Camryn will pull together and eventually start to organize. The personal images she'll leave for her girls; there are so many screenshots, duplicate photos, and silly videos, that she has no desire to comb through them herself.

Camryn repeats this process for the photos on her phone, but her folders include personal, family, and reference. There are photos of things she would like to find more information on, or articles she would like to read, but the rest of the spontaneous screenshots can be deleted.

Finally, Camryn puts a reminder on her calendar to back up the photos from all the phones every two months. She knows she could probably set up an additional cloud backup, but Camryn likes having this manual reminder to take ownership of photos she knows are precious.

 Jade

Jade's children have drifted through various activities throughout their school years, and she has tons of photos to prove it. Now she doesn't know what to do with all of them. She usually captures events with her phone, but her husband uses various cameras over time, and many of his images are attached to emails. Jade worries—how will her children ever look back on these fun times when there is no single place to look?

Searching online, Jade decides to make some photo books for her kids as Christmas presents. First, she determines what time period in their lives to cover. This helps her organize the photos and think through what books she can make. Her son went to the same summer camp for more than ten years, and the camp emailed pictures every day. Her daughter had seasons of dancing school with digital pictures provided. It would be nice to make a book of each.

Once Jade decides on her books, it becomes easier to make folders on her computer for each topic and start collecting photos from everywhere (phones, cameras, cloud accounts, emails, and texts). With so many, it's overwhelming to pull all these photos together in one place. But as Jade starts to review the photos, she keeps an eye out for only the "best"—ones featuring her kids, action shots, group photos, and portraits.

Jade starts by practicing with her daughter's dancing school book, as it has the least photos. Jade uses the online photo book software, which automatically places the pictures on the pages. She then flips through each page and makes minor adjustments. Jade can scoot photos around to feature her daughter, as well as add captions for details she feels will be memorable.

When she is finally done, she asks her husband to take a look for any redundant photos. Once Jade removes them, they agree the book looks great.

With this experience, Jade is motivated to continue and tackle her son's many camp photos. She keeps the books simple and takes advantage of an online sale to save money on printing. Jade is excited that this could be one of the most incredible Christmas presents she could give.

Harper

Harper appreciates that her parents decided to take all their loose pictures to their warehouse store to get scanned. Not having tubs of loose photos in her basement saves a lot of room. However, Harper now has a box of DVDs with tons of digital pictures in no particular order, with no recognizable names. All the photos have random numeric titles automatically given to them by the scanning software. In some ways Harper feels this is as frustrating as sifting through a physical tub of loose photos.

Harper reaches out to her siblings to see if they can share the effort to organize the photos. She ships each of them a batch of DVDs to review, and her brother sets up a cloud space to collaborate. Harper makes folders by decade and year, stretching back into the 1930s.

They plan to take a first pass at this digital organization by loading them into the cloud and into the approximate year. They keep a running chat on their phones about their progress.

Over time, Harper thinks they are turning a bit competitive in their efforts!

It is difficult not to get distracted by photos posted by her siblings. Some she has not seen in years, while some she doesn't remember at all. They text each other comments about the crazy fashions and hairstyles they encounter. Harper feels they are connecting more than they usually do in their daily lives.

She's not sure what their next step will be, but Harper is enjoying pulling their digital collection together to share with all their families.

Nadia

Nadia originally dove into creating a baby scrapbook for their daughter, and it's mostly done. However, she had barely started her son's scrapbook when she realized she couldn't keep up. Now Nadia is frustrated she has two incomplete scrapbooks, in addition to thousands of digital files.

Nadia realizes the scrapbook approach is not for her. She thinks about all the steps it already took to create the pages she has, from printing digital photos to cropping them, finding the correct page elements, and gluing everything down. She doesn't see where she would find the time to keep this going throughout her kids' younger years, but she still wants them to enjoy these photos.

Nadia's wife suggests finding a digital solution, since that reflects their life—they shoot digital photos. Nadia looks around the web until she finds a digital frame, to which they can send their photos directly from their phones. When setting it up, Nadia finds it easy to load the images and organize them as she wishes. She places the frame on a lower table so the kids can see the images. Both children frequently gather to "watch" their faces go by in the frame.

Nadia finds herself pulling photos together by theme and putting them on the digital frame. Whether it's Valentine's Day, the Fourth of July, Halloween, Christmas, or birthdays, it's fun to see what the kids looked like on that day one year prior.

As the holidays roll around, Nadia thinks this digital frame can be the perfect gift for both sets of grandparents. To load them, she points both frames to identical batches of photos, and then wraps the gifts. The grandparents simply plug in the frame, connect it to their home Wi-Fi, and immediately see the pictures. What a hit! After the holidays, Nadia enjoys putting new photos onto the frames without telling anyone, so the latest photos are always a surprise. What a fun and easy way to enjoy all these digital photos!

Takeaway

Digital photos are easily captured, but can be overwhelming to manage. It takes time to work through the chaos, and a professional may help, but the end result can bring joy to the entire family.

What's one small step you can take today?

3

Using Everything

The Challenge

My house is bursting at the seams with stuff, but it isn't anything I need at any given moment. I'm shopping to make sure we have what we need, but is it now too much? Why do I feel the need to overstock our home?

Jade's Story

I am out shopping daily. Whether it is food at the grocery store, toiletries at the drugstore, clothing, or home items, it seems like shopping is my part-time job.

However, I look around and we are not lacking. There is food on the shelves and in the refrigerator. The bathrooms seem to have tons of products, and there is no bare spot in the house.

I don't want to spend my time this way. I want to focus on my spiritual practice in my spare time. Why am I always out shopping? What do we so desperately need? What am I doing wrong? Is this just a habit?

Before COVID quarantine, I wondered if this was how I would always spend my time, losing five to six hours a week in stores. When shopping became limited, I began to really think about these activities.

Taking Action

Do you want to shift from "reactive" shopping and mindless online ordering? Try challenging yourself by going through different rooms and surveying what products you have. Whether it's the kitchen, pantry, bathroom, basement, or garage, bringing everything out of cabinets and storage bins allows you to "shop" at home and get creative in using the products you already have.

Kitchen: Figure out a week's worth of lunch from what exists in the cabinets today. Scan through recipes and figure out what you can work with:

- Whip together two to three days' worth of egg salad.

- Cook a pot of rice and separate it into containers. Pour a can of soup over each and add chicken or beef when ready to eat.

- Grill several chicken breasts simultaneously, then chop up and freeze the pieces to use anytime.

- Make a batch of homemade cookies and freeze some for later.

- Bake rolls with dinner and use extra for mini sandwiches.

Keep up the challenge until the next weekly shopping order.

If you have one-off ingredients (one extra can of pumpkin puree? Two jars of pumpkin spice?), see what it takes to whip up something new (whipped pumpkin pie), and only add those remaining ingredients to the list.

Bathroom: Pull out the entire collection of hairstyling and skin-care products from under the sink, in the closet, or in other bathrooms—everything that may or may not get used. Separate them into your favorite products, the ones you tried but didn't like, and ones that didn't perform well for you. Divide the products into the ones you love and would use before going out for a special occasion versus the ones that will do the trick for everyday use. Do not buy anything at the store until all bottles are empty.

Other ways to reduce the clutter

ReUse Shops: Look for shops specializing in household reuse items. These stores may focus more on household items than furniture. Try pulling everything out of kitchen cabinets and drawers, and you can quickly find unused kitchen gadgets and excess coffee mugs. You can drop off your items at many stores and pick up cash on the spot. The trick is leaving without purchasing anything else!

ReUse Communities online: There are many online communities with rules outlining local boundaries. By posting pictures and prices of items online, other people can post what they would like to purchase.

You have to confirm sales in the order that people have posted and then coordinate the day and time for picking up the cash purchase. Some sites have a "Porch Pickup" feature (leave it out and the purchaser leaves cash). Some local police stations have created a few "transaction" parking spaces in their lot to make a sale in a safe spot (to keep people from coming to your home). Some websites will provide local pickup and delivery with electronic payment, so the seller and buyer never meet.

Anything from excess exercise equipment to outdoor furniture and piles of children's books are easily sold this way. Take a walk around your home: What would you post for sale if you could get cash for it?

Donate: Do the homework on various donation places to learn more about who and how they benefit, then pick one you believe in. Some organizations have drop-off locations; others will pick up at your door (leaving you a receipt so you can itemize your donation for your taxes).

Ways to Get Started

Although you may want to tackle all the clutter immediately—especially if you are stuck at home—tackling one area at a time will create quicker results and reduce the chance of losing interest and leaving a mess. Small steps are the best first steps.

Camryn

Camryn always feels she is drowning in clutter, since her apartment is small, and the girls accumulated a lot of stuff as little kids. However, now she sees piles of books, toys, and dolls that her girls are no longer interested in, but still have life left in them.

She challenges them to pull out of their room every item that doesn't hold their interest anymore. Camryn sets up a spot under a window and lets the girls take pictures of each item individually with their phones. Camryn looks at some local online ReUse pages and finds one to join that sells similar items. She takes note of the book and toy prices for reference.

One Saturday morning, she and the girls sit together, and Camryn posts each item with a fair price on the website. They spend most of the afternoon getting various items bagged and ready for pickup. By the end of the day, they've earned a small profit, which Camryn splits between the girls. It's fun to be their own little online store. Camryn's older daughter pledges to dig deeper in her room for other potential "moneymakers."

Jade

The kids often moan there is nothing to eat in the house because food is not jumping out at them from the refrigerator or pantry, ready-made. Jade finds this really frustrating, and it adds to the anxiety she feels about constantly shopping. Since her kids are older, Jade gives them an exercise to make them think twice about saying they need something from the grocery store.

First, during the weekend, she asks both kids to develop four days' worth of lunches for school based on everything they currently have at home. She helps pull essential ingredients from the pantry and refrigerator and lets them work together on a plan. They can prep lunches as they go and also write down meals that can be made later in the week.

Jade expects whining and complaining that there is "nothing" to eat, but the kids quickly get to work and develop a plan for eight lunches! She was so happy she said they could both buy pizza at school on Friday for their lunch. Now Jade has a list of acceptable lunches the kids can eat (for future reference) and the exact ingredients she needs (to help her plan ahead for groceries).

Harper

Harper feels she is a whiz at meal planning, but she gets easily frustrated when something she needs disappears from the kitchen. Whether it's bread or frozen chicken fingers, she usually doesn't know she needs more until she tries to use it.

Harper decides to start a regular paper grocery list on the side of the refrigerator. If someone uses the last of an item, they have to write it down. Then, as her grocery shopping day gets closer, she challenges the kids to find something already in the kitchen that makes a good substitute. Out of bread? Put their usual sandwich in a tortilla wrap. Ate all the chips? Pre-popped air popcorn makes a good snack. Soon enough, she sees the kids start to reach for normally unused items.

Over three weeks, there is a good kitchen "cleanout" of previously ignored food items. Harper feels better at the grocery store knowing they have used what they have and she knows exactly what she needs to purchase.

Nadia

Nadia admits it is time to reduce the number of baby items in the house. Her son is a toddler, and they are not having any more children, so the infant items have to go. It seems like they are drowning in baby paraphernalia!

Nadia sends her daughter on a scavenger hunt around the house to find anything that seems like a "baby" item—piles of onesies left in the guest bedroom, blankets and burp cloths in the hall closet, various booties, and more. Meanwhile, Nadia and her wife continue the hunt in both of the kids' bedrooms.

Pulling everything together is almost overwhelming—and they didn't even include the baby furniture!

Nadia and her wife separate items into piles (clothes, toys, various baby accessories) and take pictures with their phones. She's happy to pay it forward, so they text pictures to friends they know are expecting to see who might want some free items. They donate some remaining items and sell the bigger crib and changing table online. Now, with a bit of unplanned money and more free space, they purchase a toddler bed for their son's room, spending nothing out of pocket.

Takeaway

It is tough to find the right products for your home and not create unnecessary waste. Products, toys, and books all have life cycles that eventually end. Taking the time to focus on giving up what is no longer helpful, plus engaging with charities and the community, can be great teaching tools for kids. Ask them "why buy new?" and explain the benefit of finding the same thing from someone else. You can help them learn to respect your wallet and their environment.

What's one small step you can take today?

4

Laundry in a Day

The Challenge

Dirty and clean laundry has consumed our living space as well as my mind. I am never free of it, and I'm alone in this struggle within my house.

Nadia's Story

It is sad for me to say it, but laundry is constantly on my mind. With two little kids, it seems like laundry is "always going." I know this is just a fact of life—it's not like I'm having to wash my clothes in a creek. But the constant cycle of laundry is getting under my skin.

Literally every day of the week, I do a load or two—my wife isn't here to help. Piles of laundry to fold are everywhere: bedrooms, family room. Some days I think I'm getting ahead. But there is no "ahead" in an endless cycle. Lately, it feels like suffocating pressure. I don't want to complain but I am complaining. I seriously need a laundry makeover.

Taking Action

Laundry is a fact of life. In a home, someone often not only does their own laundry but also others'. The larger the family, and the more activities (especially sports), the more to tackle. But there are some steps to bring control to the endless laundry rollercoaster.

Make your laundry room or area work for you.

- A laundry area can be unappreciated. Whether in a closet, mudroom, or basement, high-tech laundry appliances are shoved into a drab space without any other decor. Providing the room with an opportunity to shine can help. Paint a bright color on the walls, find some cute laundry-themed wallpaper or pictures, or build a "collage" of children's artwork on the wall.

- Make sure to put brighter bulbs in the light fixtures, throw a rug down, and even add a speaker for some upbeat music.

Finally, ensure adequate shelving for storage and a rack system to quickly hang up items.

Figure out your priorities.

A big choice is to confine laundry efforts to one specific day of the week. Then, figure out who's responsible: If your kids are older, hand some tasks to them. Here are some ways to get more organized:

- Make all laundry baskets identical, so there is no need to keep track of who has what basket.
- Let go of the "whitest whites," except for special occasion clothes (including eliminating whites for kids). Bright white socks are not critical in life.
- Do one child's entire load simultaneously: no separating, except for heavily-used sports wear. In, out, and back to the bedrooms in one round.
- Hang and fold items as they come out of the dryer only. No setting aside a basket "to be folded."

Delegate, delegate, delegate.

- Separate as you go: Do you and your spouse have whites, office clothes, casual clothes, and heavier fabrics (canvas or denim)? Put out baskets for each type, or use a rolling divided hamper. The baskets will provide a visual to determine which loads need to be tackled on Saturday (office clothes, workout clothes) and what can maybe wait a week (only one pair of jeans in the jeans/shorts basket).
- Kid responsibility: kids have to bring their laundry down on Saturday mornings with their hangers from the week in the basket.

- No basket = no clean clothes
- No hangers = nothing hung up to return to their room
- The kids have to take their clean clothes back up on Saturday, and everything must be put away no later than Sunday before bed.

Everyone has different hangers:

- Mom's clothes: thin velvety ones
- Husband's clothes: white plastic hangers
- Older kids: black plastic hangers
- Younger kids: smaller, child-sized white ones

Seems excessive? A little, but this means if someone sees their clothes on their hanger in the laundry room—take them! If someone is running out of hangers, was there a recent influx of clothes (birthday, holidays, back-to-school shopping)? Maybe it's time to review the closet to see what can be donated.

- Most importantly, there is a list in the laundry room cabinet of HOW TO DO THE LAUNDRY. This information is not top-secret or sacred. If someone needs a mid-week load done, ANYONE can tackle their own laundry!
- Relegate washing household items to a different day.
- Sheets, towels, kitchen towels, rugs, or anything else needing to be cleaned can be tackled on a Friday or Sunday. Kids aged ten and up can take over sheets and towel duty. Sometimes it takes a bit of reminding, but by Sunday night sheets need to be back on the beds, and towels back in the bathrooms.

Ways to Get Started

Creating a specific time to focus on laundry, coupled with clear identification of items and expectations about helping out can reduce the load (of both laundry and pressure!).

Camryn

The one thing Camryn dreads about the weekend is laundry. She already tries to keep loads "going" during the week and hates when she forgets, leaving one sitting. But she's tired when she gets home from work, and it takes all weekend to get laundry done. Between sorting, washing, and folding, by the time it is finally put away, there is already more laundry waiting. She's decided it's time to spread the "laundry wisdom" to her girls.

Looking at their schedules, she identifies one night a week that each of her daughters seems routinely free. She then assigns each of them a "laundry night." This is their one chance for the week to get their clothes washed, dried, and put away. If they miss their night, they cannot do laundry until their next designated night. Camryn knows this sounds extreme, but she also realizes that if her girls start running out of clothes, it will get their attention.

Looking around her tiny laundry room, Camryn decides to change the light bulbs in the ceiling fixture to something brighter. She's shocked by how much this improves working in the room. She also takes out miscellaneous items consuming space so her girls can have all the room they need. It is a small but subtle transformation.

On the first "designated" laundry night, she brings both girls into their tiny laundry room and talks them through what to do. Camryn also shows the girls the directions posted inside the cabinet. With this reference, they cannot forget how to get laundry going. The first month is a little rough with the girls trying to remember their designated night. Camryn continues blocking them from using the washer and dryer on the weekend as she does the rest of the laundry. Soon enough, Camryn finds her weekend laundry loads becoming more manageable, and she finally enjoys some laundry breathing room.

Jade

Jade always forgets to do the sheets, towels, and other miscellaneous laundry around the house. It is such a chore to get all the clothes done, the rest slips her mind. When she does remember, she scrambles to get everything washed. Jade is feeling guilty—like this is the measure of a bad homemaker.

Her kids have already been doing their own laundry off and on for a year. Jade wants to make this a formal routine. She assigns all bedsheets to her son and all bath towels to her daughter. Jade also sets a timeframe every week that this (along with their clothes) must be complete (or they could lose an electronic device). As expected, this plan is met with a lot of resistance.

Jade starts painting the picture for her kids of being on their own, having their own place, and what it will take to keep it clean. As they start thinking this through, the kids realize taking responsibility is a sign of being "older" and honestly, it doesn't take that much time. Jade feels that even if the kids forget their chore one week, they are keeping up with the tasks better than she had been by herself, so assigning the chores benefits everyone.

Harper

Harper has laundry down to a science. Walking into the laundry room just as the cycles are ending is practically instinctual at this point. However, she ends up with huge piles in baskets, almost too heavy to move, let alone get back to the right bedrooms to put away. She notices that sometimes her kids just dress themselves directly out of the basket—they never make it to putting clothes away.

Harper decides to invest in a hanger system to get things out of baskets and immediately hung in closets. She puts all her kids' clothes on white plastic hangers, and her and her husband's items on black hangers. This makes it easy for everyone to see what to grab and take back to their closets.

She then starts putting clothes on hangers immediately out of the dryer including all shirts, pants, leggings, jeans, and even shorts (using clip hangers). Suddenly, the baskets are nearly empty, only holding underclothes, socks, and pajamas for drawers. Harper lays the appropriate pile of clothes (on hangers) across the baskets and forces her kids to return it all to their rooms and put everything away. She stands over each child for a bit explaining how fast and easy this is now.

Harper's youngest daughter has difficulty hanging stuff in her closet—it's jammed with clothes. Harper takes this time to weed out the myriad of clothes her daughter has outgrown. Suddenly, Harper has more hangers and her daughter has more room in the closet. This becomes a ritual after Sunday night's dinner. Everyone gathers their clothes and puts everything away before they prepare for school on Monday. Harper feels better not having to constantly complain that she works hard on the laundry, but it never gets put away.

 Nadia

Nadia has been looking for tips for all aspects of organizing, but when it comes to laundry, she figures it is a lost cause. With two small children, the clothes are small, but the volume is large. The worst part is how dumb she feels sitting in her own closet sorting out what to wash, because she and her wife just throw all dirty clothes into one pile.

Nadia figures the kids' clothing will evolve over time, but there is something she can do now to make the chore easier. She purchases three laundry baskets and squeezes them into the space where the laundry pile normally sits. Nadia doesn't feel a need to label the baskets, but she sorts the existing laundry pile into three groups: whites, office clothes, and workout/around-the-house clothes.

Nadia shows her wife how much faster it will be to grab the basket that has the most laundry in it to wash. It won't seem like all clothes are dirty and the pile is too large for a load. Her wife thinks it is a great idea and tries to stick with it. For a couple of weeks, they have to get used to this pre-sorting activity, but Nadia relishes seeing exactly what needs to be washed before it gets out of hand.

Takeaway

It's difficult to measure the sense of relief to not see overflowing laundry baskets or piles of clothes everywhere. Consider it a parenting win knowing that when kids move out on their own, they will have a slightly better than average chance of keeping their clothes clean because they know what to do and how long it will take.

What's one small step you can take today?

5

Power Groceries

The Challenge

Dinner is the recurring headache in my day. I am unsure of what we are having until it is about time to prepare it. Usually, I don't have what we need and am running to the store or ordering restaurant delivery. Both our waistlines and wallets feel this madness.

Jade's Story

I run to the store almost every day for something I forgot or something we need for dinner. Most days, I'm not sure what's for dinner until late afternoon. Then I am scouring cabinets, the refrigerator, and the freezer for instant inspiration. It's embarrassing to make my family settle for cereal. There seems to be chaos around groceries and dinner that I have not gotten under control, and it is wearing me out. Hearing the kids complain there is nothing to eat adds to this anxiety.

With this last-minute approach—just making the quickest and easiest decision—I know I'm not making healthy choices for my family. I need a better strategy.

Taking Action

Planning can certainly take the stress out of dinner, but it does not have to be a one-person chore. By checking the family calendar and determining the evening plans for the week, it becomes easier to figure out which meals make sense on which days. Consider creating (or pulling from your grocery store ordering site) a printed list of your family's everyday grocery items and posting it in the kitchen. Everyone can circle what they have run out of OR add something new.

An electronic way to tackle this same activity is the website Plan to Eat. This site makes it easy to snip a recipe online and add it to your database. When it is time for meal planning, simply drag and drop the name of a meal or dish onto the included meal calendar. The site will then generate a grocery list of everything needed for all meals. You can remove items you already have, then add on some staples you always purchase (beverages, snacks, fruit, vegetables, paper products, etc). In a short amount of time, your list is ready.

Set aside some time to search for fresh recipe ideas on the internet and load them into the system with one click instead of typing. Recipes can be put into categories that you create—for example, dinner categories could include:

- Crockpot/Instant pot
- Vegetarian
- Fish
- Meat
- One-pan
- Kid favorites

Whether with paper or an online system, leverage a standard shopping list to generate what you need for each grocery trip. Have older children? Give them the Plan to Eat app on their device and let them load their favorite meals on certain days. Share the planning!

Many grocery stores now offer an on-demand grocery shopping experience. Use your list to select everything needed online, then pick up the groceries at a designated time while you stay in your car. These grocery sites save all previous orders, so reordering is efficient.

Ways to Get Started

A method that works for you and your family is key to making the meal-planning process straightforward. You can even consider adding in plans for Saturday breakfast or Sunday brunch!

Camryn

Camryn feels she and her daughters eat out or order in more than she prefers. When she gets home from work, she just doesn't have the energy to figure out dinner. She knows cooking for the three of them is not a lot, but it seems momentous after 6:00 pm.

Camryn is looking to bring some order to this effort. She sits down with the girls and asks about their favorite meals (at home and when they go out). With that list, she charges the girls with finding as many of these recipes online as possible. When they find ones they like, they print and assemble their own custom cookbook in a binder.

Her oldest daughter is tasked with finding the common ingredients across the recipes and checking to see what they already have in the cabinets: things like olive oil, salt, pepper, and other basics. Camryn works to assemble the remainder of the ingredients list for the next five nights of dinners.

Thinking about everything she dreads when it comes to dinners at home, Camryn realizes it is the trip to the store, then hauling all the groceries to their apartment, that she loathes. Camryn decides to look up her local grocery store online and try out their delivery service. She orders more significant amounts of essential items, plus ingredients for the designated meals and other basics. There is a small fee for the delivery, but Camryn is surprised at the sheer relief she feels when the groceries arrive at her door!

She and the girls rearrange in the kitchen to make all these supplies fit—and now are ready for the week. Camryn takes the recipes out of the binder and hangs them on the refrigerator. She is prepared for their week of dining in (and keeps one night set aside to order out).

Jade

Jade knows that to move towards actual dinner planning she will need everyone's help. First, she delegates to her husband the signup and setup of the Plan to Eat app. As he does, she and the kids talk about the kinds of meals they enjoy (or dislike!). Her husband chimes in with grilling options for them to consider. Jade also asks about some go-to foods that would work if coming together for dinner is not an option.

Jade checks online recipe sites for ideas, drifting towards crockpot, one-pan, and other simple meal types. She quickly masters adding the recipes to the app, then makes up her own recipes to account for grilling or nights of canned soup. After noting everyone's weekday evening plans on their family calendar, Jade finds it doesn't take long to develop a grocery list for two weeks of meals.

With her grocery list in hand, Jade decides to commit to one weekly trip to the store. She keeps thinking she will forget something, but her list accounts for recipe ingredients and all the basics.

In addition, Jade finds that heading to the kitchen at 5:30 to start dinner no longer brings the anxiety it had previously. Jade enjoys preparing a meal for her family. After a few months, she takes her unused cookbooks to the secondhand store to sell.

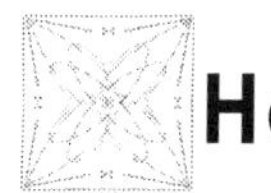

Harper

Harper has no problem making home-cooked meals daily—she doesn't like the expense of eating out. However, week after week, it takes her forever to make a grocery list. She prefers a paper list for the store, but she writes down many of the same items every week.

Harper types up a list with everything she considers a regular purchase. At the end, she leaves some lines to write in additional groceries. She keeps the printed list in front of her all week and asks the family if there is anything they would like to add.

After a couple of weeks, Harper returns to her grocery list electronic file and moves items around to match the layout of her regular grocery store. She certainly knows her way around! Now, her trip to the store moves faster, since she no longer pauses in every aisle to scan up and down her list. Harper is proud to improve this routine activity in her life.

 Nadia

Nadia notices their regular grocery shopping is reduced to buying primarily items the kids eat. Her children are at the stage where they prefer a few common meals, and it seems she and her wife eat the same.

Nadia does not think she can face another chicken nugget dinner, so she talks to her wife about some old favorites they enjoyed cooking together before the kids came along. Nadia assembles a list of these favorites and tries for three nights a week to have "adult" dinners.

Since they are making two different meals, Nadia asks her wife to give her a hand in the kitchen: one makes their adult dinner, while the other warms and assembles the kids' meal. They begin to enjoy their time in the kitchen together. Most meals are not complex and do not take long, but they both come to the dinner table a bit more relaxed, giving the kids what they want to eat while having something a bit more special for themselves.

Takeaway

No more scrambling to figure out dinner. No more wandering around the store trying to determine what to make for the week. No more impulse ordering dinners. A planning trick or two can reduce the pressure of family dinner for everyone in the house.

What's one small step you can take today?

6

Kitchen Stations

The Challenge

Everything takes longer to do in the kitchen than I think it will as I try to find things. I thought I was organized, but my kitchen setup does not work for me or my family.

Nadia's Story

I think my wife's obsession with grilling is taking over my kitchen. Her "expertise" comes with a myriad of accessories and items, which unfortunately can't all be stored outside—not every day is a sunny grilling day where we live.

Every time she grills, she goes through every cabinet to pull all the accessories she needs. This turns into a whirlwind for me when I make dinner, since the grilling items are in almost every kitchen cabinet.

Grilling accessories are not the only things we hunt for in our kitchen. The coffee pot is by the water, but the mugs are across the kitchen by the dishwasher. Mixing bowls are in one area, but measuring cups and spoons hide somewhere else. Some single-use kitchen tools live in the top drawers, but neither of us uses them. It's frustrating that this chaos makes cooking take even longer. I know it's time to organize and consolidate. But what makes sense in a kitchen?

Taking Action

Kitchens can easily be the catch-all for many items, but if you are doing laps back and forth trying to get a meal assembled, the kitchen isn't making much sense. There are various ways to organize and create "stations" where everything you need is in one place.

Stations

Coffee & Tea: Is everything you need for morning coffee spread everywhere? Decide where the coffee pot should go and surround it with everything you need: mugs, stirrers, sweeteners, anything else that says coffee (or tea). Then get creative. Do you have a little unused desk area in the kitchen? Turn it into your coffee counter with shelves, coffee decorations, and anything else that signals "coffee brewed here."

Grilling: Are grill items taking over kitchen space? Look for a spot of empty wall space and designate that as the "grilling station." By purchasing both a base and wall cabinet that matches your kitchen or dining area, you can designate one spot for all things involved in grilling. Make sure the bottom cabinet has solid doors and adjustable shelves so all the grilling items fit. If you want, opt for more attractive wall cabinets: maybe glass fronts to show off accumulated grilling spices and rubs. Look for other items like a large ceramic container to hold the long grilling tongs, spatulas, and even fire pit roasting sticks. This container can easily be set atop the base cabinet. Suddenly one place has everything needed for a fantastic BBQ. This change provides more space in the original kitchen cabinets and allows for purging unnecessary grilling items during the transition.

Baking: Do you love to bake, but everything is spread across the kitchen? Consider changing a cabinet that only stores mixing bowls into a bakery station. Put all the mixing bowls on the lowest shelf. Use removable adhesive hooks to hang dry measuring cups, spoons, and mixing attachments inside the cabinet door. Try placing one or two liquid measuring glasses and everyday baking dishes in the cabinet. On the second shelf, place actual baking ingredients, including sugar, flour, yeast, chocolate chips, vanilla, baking mixes, parchment paper, and other go-to items. Have a standing counter mixer? If it doesn't fit in the cabinet, place it on the counter right below, plugged in and ready. Next to it, keep a jar for all mixing spoons and spatulas.

Do other items fit the same description? Snack bags taking over the pantry? Everyday dishes, glasses, and silverware far away from the dishwasher? What other "stations" can be created to centralize what you need? Utilize containers, bins, hooks, and other "organizing" items to bring all tools together, including adjusting shelves and leveraging baskets.

Ways to Get Started

Think about how you truly use your kitchen and create zones or spots to do that work. This can make cooking faster and more efficient.

Camryn

At least once a month, Camryn's daughters get the urge to bake. While Camryn is doing something else in the apartment, she comes into the kitchen to see the girls climbing all over the counters to gather everything they need. Camryn realizes this is crazy, and her kitchen setup makes it hard for the girls to do something they enjoy. She can also predict a bowl or baking dish crashing to the floor because they're out of reach.

Once the girls are done baking one afternoon, Camryn has them wash everything and set all their items on the counter. Together, they empty a lower cabinet, where they load all their baking items. As they work, the girls think of additional items that make sense to include, like food coloring and cookie cutters.

Camryn digs up a basket to hold measuring spoons, spatulas, and other tools to place on one cabinet shelf. Finally, they set their stand mixer directly below this cabinet. The girls are so excited to have everything in one place and easily accessible. It also creates one place for Camryn to check if they are low on any common ingredients.

They consolidate the items they removed from the lower cabinet into other places and hang potholders on the wall behind the mixer. Camryn figures baking will become more frequent now that the girls have everything they need in one place.

Jade

Jade doesn't know why they have snacks all over the kitchen. Over time cookies end up in one spot, chips in another, and jars of unopened dip are across the kitchen. Sometimes she finds two of the same things in two places, as her husband and children don't realize the other exists. This drives Jade crazy, because it makes her think they are out of something when they're actually not.

To top it off, there is literally a snack war in the house. Anytime someone dares eat someone else's food, the accusations begin. The entire situation is getting on her nerves.

Jade decides to make a "snack closet." She takes advantage of the many pantry shelves and uses three large, clear, plastic food storage bins with solid lids. Jade writes each of her family members' names across the bins with a marker, dumps that person's favorite snack in their storage bin, and places it in the pantry with a corresponding unopened bag of the same snack behind it. Next to the three bins, she puts a basket labeled "family snacks" for things like cookies or brownies if someone baked, or popcorn kernels for family movie night.

Finally, she tapes a lined piece of paper inside the pantry door and adds a pencil on a piece of string next to it. Jade brings the family together and shows them their "personal" snack containers with the rule of not touching any other person's bin. She also shows them where to write down if they are running low on their snack (or want something different). Now Jade only has to look at the list to know what to get at the store. Finally, she creates a caveat—if the item is not on the list, she is not getting it at the store. Her family is responsible for determining when to refill snacks; she will not take her time to figure it out.

Harper

When Harper and her family first moved into their home, she organized her kitchen for what made sense at the time. But as the family grows and adds things, Harper notices that where she originally stored things no longer makes sense.

Harper opens all her kitchen wall cabinets and stands back to look. She has many cooking supplies next to the refrigerator, which is nowhere near the island where she makes meals. The dishes and glasses are in the cabinet furthest away from the kitchen table and even the dishwasher. Harper didn't realize that glasses and mugs are migrating and scattered in several spots.

Harper grabs a piece of paper and draws columns on it to match the number of wall cabinets. She starts writing down what makes more sense. Dishes and glasses could go between the dishwasher and the dining room table. Cooking supplies could go directly behind the spot at the island where she works.

Harper then draws a horizontal line across the lower part of the columns, opens all of the drawers, and notices some drawer shuffling is in order. Silverware needs to move closest to the dishes, with cooking utensils moving behind her at the island. Harper determines the junk drawer needs to shift to the last drawer before exiting the kitchen.

With this plan, Harper is surprised how quickly she moves things around. As she works, she finds a few items she no longer uses and sets them aside to donate to her church. Before she knows it, everything is tucked away again.

When Harper starts making dinner, she realizes how much muscle memory her body has when reaching for something. She finds herself traveling numerous times to the wrong cabinet out of habit. Harper figures if she has problems remembering the new layout, her family will certainly struggle. She posts sticky notes on the front of every cabinet and drawer to signal changes. It takes a week, but Harper and her family adapt to the new organization. When it comes to her children emptying the dishwasher, consolidating all the dishes, glasses, and silverware close to the dining table and dishwasher is an absolute winner.

Nadia

Nadia has to confront her wife about all the grilling tools and supplies taking over their kitchen. She can barely reach the spices because of all the bottles of grilling rubs and mixtures in the cabinet. Long-handled grilling tools are jammed into any spot where they fit. Various grilling pans are piled on top of regular baking sheets.

As they discuss it, they recognize the need to consolidate, but do not want to spend much money on the effort. Nadia and her wife try to figure out what they can use to solve their storage issue. They laugh when they both set their eyes on a curio cabinet in the dining room. It has hardly anything in it since they do not collect trinkets, but it is part of the dining room set they inherited from Nadia's parents. They haul the cabinet to the garage and dig up paint to make it the same ivory color as their kitchen cabinets. They bring it back in and tuck it away between the end of their kitchen and their sliding glass patio door.

Nadia leaves it to her wife to load up the grilling cabinet. She pulls grill items out of every cabinet and creates a pile on the kitchen table for her wife to sort through. When she returns an hour later, Nadia finds a charming grilling station ready to use. Spices are lined up across the top two shelves on clear display. Long-handled baskets and trays are standing up with their handles easy to grab. There is also an old, tall ceramic plant pot filled with grilling utensils. Other miscellaneous grilling items are tucked below in the solid cabinet, out of sight.

Nadia is thrilled to go through the kitchen, open cupboards and drawers, and see they have been returned to their original intended use.

Takeaway

A kitchen is a space in the home that can quickly expand beyond its original purpose. With so many things tucked out of sight, it is difficult to determine if the original setup still makes sense as the kitchen evolves. Taking a step back to reevaluate can create efficiencies for everyone.

What's one small step you can take today?

7

SELF-CARE: Essential Oils

The Challenge

I want to move to healthier practices for physical and mental well-being, and steer clear of over-the-counter medicines and unhealthy chemicals when I can. I'm not sure how to start this journey for my family.

Jade's Story

I think about how my house is filled with soaps and cleaners that I realize can be harsh for us and our environment. I know I hand out over-the-counter pain and sinus pills as my family needs them. However, I often think about making a shift to healthier solutions.

I purchased an essential oil "starter kit" that includes some basic oils, and I would like to learn how to leverage them. I'm impressed with moms who reach for these instead of chemicals for cleaning and health care. I don't want to make things complicated, but I feel guilty about using possibly unhealthy products.

Taking Action

Utilizing essential oils is a tradition and therapy that is thousands of years old. These oils are pulled from plants and can be used for anything from relaxation to stimulation. Today, there are so many oils, it can be challenging to know what could work for which ailment (besides lavender for sleep, which seems to be a standard health tip). A great way to begin is with a starter kit of basic essential oils.

Learning More

It can take a bit of time to research what goes into a quality essential oil and how to use it. Most essential oil brands provide websites full of information, and plenty of books and blogs can explain their uses. Other resources include support in private online user groups, where someone well-versed in essential oil use can answer various questions. However, you should not abandon prescribed medication for essential oils without discussing with your doctor.

Blending

As you learn more, consider blending oils for greater effectiveness. Rollerballs allow mixing and quick application for things like allergy season symptoms or helping a child focus. There are a variety of practical applications to explore.

Convenience

As you continue your journey, using essential oils is helpful if you place them in the right areas.

- Using oil for settling a stomach? Keep it stored with existing medicines.
- Leveraging an oil for headaches? Again, in the medicine cabinet or even a purse.
- Want to relax? A bottle with an oil blend by the bathtub.
- Trying to perk up a gray day? Keeping a blend of citrus oil handy in your office desk drawer can help.
- Getting tired in the afternoons? A centrally located rollerball bottle of oil can be smoothed onto your wrists to perk up.
- Looking to improve your skin? Keep oils with your skincare products, and blend a drop or two into existing moisturizers.
- Need to add some zest to recipes? Tuck a bottle of lemon or oregano essential oil in the kitchen cabinet.
- Using oils for cleaning products? Keep some located with the spray bottles and other cleaners to refill when running low.
- Want to keep bugs away outside, but not use harsh bug spray? A combination of oils can do the trick and be stored alongside sunscreen and other outside items.

Oils in easy reach are a great way to stop grabbing other options. However, follow the directions on storing oils properly, plus take note on which oils can be ingested versus which ones should only be used topically.

Travel

When planning to travel, small pouches of vials are available. These can be filled with oils to help tummy or sinus problems, stop germs from spreading, and even soothe achy legs. The Transportation Security Authority (TSA) must review the pouch in airports, but the vials are small enough to get through security.

Reminders

Capturing and printing suggested uses and blends can inspire you continue utilizing existing products or add new ones. Taping up blend recipes inside cabinets where current products are stored helps keep that focus.

Ways to Get Started

With research, advice, and trial and error, working with essential oils can bring traditional relaxation and restorative experiences.

 Jade

Since she has the starter kit of oils, Jade purchases an oil diffuser. She isn't sure what to put in it, so she searches online for an easy oil combination that sounds fresh, but utilizes what she has. Jade positions the diffuser on a counter, as the kitchen transitions into the family room, and is amazed at how quickly the gentle and calming scent moves through their common space. As everyone arrives home, they comment on how clean and relaxing the smell is.

With that positive reaction, Jade starts researching blend ideas for a gentle, all-purpose cleaning product that also smells beautiful. She starts a file on her computer of suggestions to try.

Personally, Jade is also interested in how the oils could help with common issues like headaches and sinus congestion. She knows she will try that type of use first before sharing with her family. But finding a healthy alternative to some over-the-counter solutions makes sense to her.

Takeaway

Research is important when making any changes to the family's environment and health. Consulting with a physician is also critical. Quality of ingredients and expert suggestions can help transform your approach to healthy living.

What's one small step you can take today?

8

Digitizing Print Photos

The Challenge

I seem to inherit so many photos and old albums from family members, yet I don't enjoy them. There are tubs and tubs of photos, overwhelming piles in no order, that make me resent this legacy being dumped on me.

Camryn's Story

Somehow, I have my family's photo collection, so my shelves are full of these sizable, three-ring binder albums. The photos are on sticky pages with clear protectors (that are not protecting). Photos are changing colors and starting to slip out as the glue gives up. I don't spend a lot of time looking back at these books. It's like they are on my shelves for posterity's sake because my family has always had them.

My mom did a wonderful job capturing our family memories in these albums, but now it feels overwhelming. On top of that, it's not like my brother and sister have access to them. I'm trying hard not to see these as a burden, but I'm annoyed that the little space I have is absorbed by these legacy books. The responsibility of these albums leaves me feeling guilty and stuck with this inheritance.

Taking Action

Family photos are usually prized possessions: the first things anyone wants to save in a fire. Charitable organizations rush into hurricane-impacted cities to teach people how to dry out and preserve damaged photos. They are important to us!

However, years of accumulating pictures in various formats and collections passing from generation to generation can create an overwhelming mess. This disorganization can invoke both frustration (not able to find anything) and guilt (these photos should be cherished).

With technology today, people are considering digitizing their print photo collection for backup, space, and ease of use. Whether it is boxes of loose photos or all those binders of sticky pages, the shift to digital legacy photos can be a huge undertaking.

The best approach is to organize the physical before going digital, so you don't replicate chaos in your collection. Do you have lots of sticky page albums or flip pages with a photo inserted in each? What about those time-consuming scrapbooks? As much as we enjoy them, they take up significant space and are difficult to share with non-local family and friends.

Reviewing What You Have

The first thing you can do is review these books with one thought in mind: Which pictures are the best? We all printed many photos, particularly in the 1970s and 1980s, but not all were winners—time to curate, so every image you save tells the story. Some questions to ask before moving forward with these items include:

- How far back do the images go?
- How many are loose? A shoebox full? Tubs full?
- How many albums are there?
- How many home movies are there?
- How many slides are there (number of trays)?
- Is there a good chance the albums and the loose photos/ slides are the same?

Loose photos, home movies, and slides can all be sorted by decade to help prioritize what should be made digital. This effort will help determine if the volume warrants assistance from either a personal photo organizer, a transfer studio (for the film, slides, and VHS tapes), or a print-scanning company.

Albums are more complicated. To make a decision on how to convert these pages, start by reviewing an album with a pad of small sticky notes. To narrow down photos worth scanning, place the sticky note over the pictures (on the protective cover) you are not interested in. When finished, you can quickly review the photos you didn't include and see if you are missing any parts of your legacy information. When you are finished with a book, this activity will help you in two ways:

- Look at all the sticky notes you have applied. Do the remaining photos seem like too many? Are there enough images for the time frame of the album?

- Review the unselected photos (covered with a sticky note). Do you feel comfortable leaving them out of your digital collection?

Make it fun by reviewing an album with a friend or relative or at a family gathering. If missing, make annotations on the sticky note of the date, location, and people. Know you are taking the first step in keeping your memories alive for future generations in a way they can genuinely use.

Pulling It All Together

The next step in preparing to go digital with your photos is to decide how to scan them. There are several options:

- Removing photos. Remove all photos tagged for scanning. In some cases, the page adhesive destroys pictures, or the glue can be so strong that the images will rip upon removal.

- The best tool for removal is a metal spatula (the kind used for clay work found in art stores). They are slim enough to slip under a photo, and the handle provides control to slide the photo off the page (like a cookie from a cookie sheet). Once removed, you or a professional scanning service can scan the images. If you plan to keep the individual prints, this is a good option. It is critical to store those prints in archival-safe boxes. The original albums (with the undesired photos) can be discarded.

- Scanning the pages as is. If you want to keep every photo, scanning the entire page is a better approach. However, this can be tedious, as all plastic covering needs to be removed from every page.

- Once scanned, the page can be saved in a digital folder by album, with a page number assigned to keep the pages in sequence. It may be easier to discard the original albums and keep only the digital pages, by replicating the entire album.

- Digitally separating the photos. Individual photos can be saved into individual photo files while still attached to the album pages. You will need to crop the preferred images to become individual files, or use scanning software that automatically selects individual photos.

- This approach is a good idea when you suspect there are other prints (not in the albums) that you will want to merge with the album photos. The individual digital images can then be stored in folders by album or topic, with the ability to add more.

Finally, naming the electronic files is critical for the final organization. Whether by year, topic, album name, or date, the file naming can make it easy to move files around, and still know exactly where they originally belong. A typical file-naming practice includes the year, month, day, possible topic, and a number for sequencing. For example:

2014_05_18_Spring Recital_01.jpg

This naming provides the date (year then month which keeps files in order), a bit about what the photos are (in this case, from the spring recital), and a number correlating to the order of photos within the event (01). The corresponding folder for these folders would include the same details without the end numbering:

2014_05_18_Spring Recital

File naming also keeps a chronological structure, even if the actual day is unknown and excluded from the file name. File renaming software can apply the naming and individual numbering in batches to speed up the process. Suddenly, a digital library can look as organized as a print library of albums.

Taming the Slides

Is a large portion of family photos on slides? These are tough to work with—both to view and enjoy easily. To get started, decide the fate of the slides first: do all the slides need to be stored more efficiently and kept OR will they be scanned and the original slides discarded?

If storing, look for safer, more effective ways to keep slides, including box systems available at archive photo supply websites. Setting aside one weekend to transfer slides out of carousels and into preservation-worthy boxes can quickly move the collection from mess to organized with a solution that takes up far less space. Save one carousel for viewing if you have the projector to do so.

Consider reviewing the slides for possible digitizing and incorporating them into family albums or files. Utilizing a hand-held slide viewer can keep you from setting up a full slide projector and screen. Once selected, there are several scanning options, from sending slides to a scanning service to renting equipment. Because slides can be so difficult to access regularly, you may bring to life images the entire family had forgotten about.

Ways to Get Started

Whether it's to gain more space or preserve family memories, tackling those piles of photos can provide peace of mind. Making some initial decisions about organizing photos and the desired result will make the path clear to begin.

Camryn

Looking over the album collection, Camryn decides to work with a personal photo organizer to tackle this project. After discussing options, she feels scanning the photos into individual picture files makes the most sense, allowing her to pull any image at any time. Plus, the organizer will transfer details written on the backs of photos into the information in the photo file, as well as color correcting photos that seem particularly faded. Camryn sets a budget to have two albums completed at a time.

Over a couple of weekends, Camryn sits with her daughters and looks through every album. They collectively decide which photos are the best and which don't need to be scanned.

Camryn realizes that once the photos are digitized, she can send a hard drive to each of her siblings so they can share the legacy photos. She reaches out to both siblings to tell them about her project, and they love the idea. They both volunteer to contribute to the cost, which makes the project go a lot faster. In the end, the organizer provides Camryn with three hard drives, so each sibling owns a copy of the collection.

Once Camryn sends the drives to her siblings, and they review the photos on their computer or TV, they truly understand the value of the effort. All three agree the physical albums are no longer needed, and tell Camryn to discard them. This decision allows Camryn to use her precious shelf space for items that invoke other special memories.

Jade

Jade and her three sisters begin talking about their family albums one weekend on the anniversary of their mom's passing. Each sister has a couple of the albums, and they wonder if that makes sense, or if one of them should be the keeper of all of them. When they each mention how many albums they have, the total adds up to twenty. That's a lot for one person to take responsibility for!

They also discuss what they could do with these albums, as they are rarely reviewed. Some albums have older pictures that, between the three of them, they do not know much about. The sisters agree the best option is to scan the album pages (all at the same resolution), and upload the files to a cloud storage solution so they can review everything online.

Knowing this can take time and effort, they decide to work backwards. Everyone has the latest of their albums scanned, since they know the details of these photos.

At their summer family reunion, they bring the albums that need more detail, and sit with the older family members to review. With sticky notes handy, Jade and her sisters can capture information and stories from relatives who know more about the people and places in the photos. As they work, more and more people gather around to listen and enjoy the progress.

Jade and her sisters scan the remaining albums and type up the corresponding notes. With everything online, they realize they now have a fully digital collection they can share that the aunts, uncles, and cousins can also enjoy.

Jade also researches how big of an external hard drive she needs to store the files they brought together. She makes a backup of everything online, which brings her and her siblings peace of mind.

Harper

Harper's parents sent her their entire slide photo collection as they scaled down and moved into assisted living. At the time, she tossed everything in the basement to deal with later. Now,

Harper decides her weekend project is to reduce the sprawl of these unwieldy photos.

By searching online, Harper finds some slide storage kits that could significantly save space. She enlists her husband to help remove all slides from carousels and load them into narrow storage boxes. These can then be labeled by topic and placed in larger preservation boxes. She can't believe how much space she saves!

Harper might not keep all the slides. But by labeling the individual boxes, she can prioritize what to scan and possibly keep.

Nadia

Since her children were born, Nadia has been taking them to a local portrait studio for formal pictures. In their first year, it was every month. After year one, she did it twice a year—on their birthday and half-birthday—to capture how fast they were changing. Now her daughter is moving to school pictures.

Nadia always has an 8x10 photo printed, which she rotates through frames on their mantle. When it is time to replace the pictures, she can slide the previous ones into an album with the same-sized pages. All these enlargements are gathered together.

However, Nadia wishes to have digital files of these photos (she never thought to include them in her packages). Nadia contacts the studio, and for a fee, she can purchase the digital files from the sessions.

Once Nadia downloads the photos, she realizes the file names are generic numbers. She groups the photos into folders by child and date. Then Nadia creates a master folder for each child, with a sub-folder for each photo shoot. She types the date of the shoots on the folder and the files, so she knows where every file belongs.

Nadia feels she can tuck the original album away, since she has everything she needs at her fingertips, plus a digital frame to showcase their photos.

Takeaway

The options to properly manage print photos are varied, but valuable. Recruiting other family members, or hiring a professional, helps get pictures into a manageable collection that can be of value to everyone in the family.

What's one small step you can take today?

9

Closet Care

The Challenge

The closets in my house are packed full, and it is impossible to find anything. I don't know if they are too cluttered, or if my closets are not designed to hold what I'm shoving in there. We are constantly looking for what we need.

Harper's Story

I have had enough of our master bedroom closet. The previous owners installed one wire-rack shelf/rod combination, which does not do the job. I keep meticulously folded piles of clothes on the shelf, but I'm worried that with all the weight from both hanging and folded clothes, it will soon rip out of the wall.

I look around at the stacks of shoeboxes, bags of extra toiletries, towels, sheets, and blankets piled in the same closet, and realize I barely use half of it because it is so hard to dig through. Even with my bins and baskets, it's difficult to find something in the closet's low light.

When I go to the hall closet to grab a jacket, I have the same challenge. We constantly shuffle jackets to get other items in and out. The vacuum cleaner is also buried, which I have to fight to set free every week.

Although these areas look somewhat neat, the underlying mess bothers me. We don't have the budget for a closet company to come in and install systems. My basic stacking isn't helping enough. I need to do something.

Taking Action

A closet commonly has only a rod or coated wire rack with a shelf incorporated. Neither of these fills the needs of a bedroom or hall closet. A remodeled closet can look expensive, but not cost a lot.

Bedroom Closets

Remodeling a master bedroom closet can be a do-it-yourself project. It takes some inspiration and homework to develop a storage design and some websites can help with this. Once you have a plan for shelves, drawers, and hanging rods, these are steps that can transform the closet:

1. Remove all wire racks and anchors.

2. Patch walls and paint the entire closet a soft color.

3. Install a four-foot (or longer) LED light fixture to cover the length of the closet.

4. Install a sensor so the light goes on and off as you enter the closet (when your hands are full of laundry baskets!).

5. Plan for one wall to be a shelf and drawer system, and one wall to be hanging racks.

6. Purchase a standard closet shelf and drawer system from a hardware or resell store (keep an eye out for ones on clearance) and install using the correct wall anchors OR utilize existing freestanding shelves and dressers.

   TIP: When installing adjustable shelves, keep the bottom shelf high enough off the ground so that laundry baskets fit into the bottom area.

7. Utilize the wire racks previously removed by cutting them in half and installing two racks for hanging clothes on the unused wall. Keep the lower row slightly shorter in length than the upper row, so there is space to hang dresses, long pants, etc.

8. Install additional small cubby shelves wherever there is room (even behind the door).

9. Install a full-length mirror in the space if warranted.

10. Install several "towel rack" poles (the kind that attach to the wall with three to four swiveling horizontal arms), which you can use to hang tank tops and camis.

11. Install hooks behind the door (on the wall) for robes, belts, ball caps, scarves, or hats.

12. Utilize slim hangers to give clothes some wiggle room, and not pack the closet so tightly.

Figuring out an inexpensive cabinet or shelving system, combined with reusing existing racks, can quickly transform a closet. Adequate lighting allows you to clearly and quickly see everything. Finding a place for everything (with only lightweight items on the wire rack shelves) can help you store more than you ever imagined.

Hall Closets

In some areas, a hall closet can be nothing more than a showcase of your extensive coat collection. It can be frustrating to jam so many coats—especially the puffy ones—into a small space. Other hall closets may be filled with sporting and outdoor equipment.

However, there is an alternative to this traditionally small space, with one pole going between two walls. Steps to transform this space include:

1. Pull everything (including the rod) out of the closet and patch any holes.

2. Paint the inside of the closet a faint, light color. Since closets seem to have low-grade paint on the walls, they become easily scuffed, and the entire closet looks dingy.

3. Mount wall hooks (the kind where there are five, two-tiered hooks across a backing, not individual hooks) around the perimeter of the closet. A small hall closet can accommodate these hook panels across the three walls at "adult" height. An additional two can be mounted (one on each side wall) at "child" height.

Suddenly there are fifty spots to hang coats! Lower hooks are perfect for empty tote bags and winter scarves. To top it off, something larger like a vacuum cleaner can slide straight into the middle—no more digging through a forest of coats to get to your cleaning tools.

Leveraging Lighting with Storage

Replacing a single bulb fixture with an LED fluorescent fixture can make a huge difference in a small space. These come in various lengths to brighten any area. In addition, adding light sensors in rooms saves energy and illuminates your path as you walk inside. Consider any room or closet where you walk in with your hands full as a candidate to switch to a sensor. The laundry room, master closet, and garage are all ideal places to start.

Have a professional electrician make any of these electrical improvements. The cost can be nominal to have an electrician walk through your home and suggest ways for you to improve your fixtures in a way that works for you and saves money.

Ways to Get Started

Targeting a little-used closet can be a great way to practice this type of remodeling before tackling more essential areas.

Camryn

Camryn is thrilled her apartment came with a closet system installed (a couple of built-in shelves for each closet). However, they are all outgrowing these shelves; there isn't enough room. Camryn takes a picture of each closet, then spends time online trying to develop ideas.

She realizes she can add another set of freestanding cubby shelves to fit below the existing shelves in both girls' closets. They select white ones to blend into the closets' existing structures. The girls opt for bright-colored cube boxes as storage bins.

Camryn's oldest daughter moves shorts and T-shirts onto these shelves and clears out a dresser drawer. This makes it easier for her to put together what to wear. Her younger daughter uses the cubby shelves for shoe storage, and puts accessories in the colorful bins. After seeing the success in both girls' rooms, Camryn thinks she should take a second look at her own closet.

Jade

Jade feels physically tired of her hall closet. Everyone shoves everything into it, with no regard for putting anything away correctly. She worries she will open the closet door one day, and everything will fall out on top of her—just like a scene from a movie.

Jade decides to pull absolutely everything out of the closet and organize items into piles according to owner. Her kids have a ton of outdoor equipment that should be in the garage. Her husband has many coats, and Jade finds long-lost gloves, hats, and scarves.

She has each owner claim their pile. The only things Jade allows back into the closet are coats. Her husband and son partner to create better storage space in the garage for all outdoor equipment. Jade and her daughter pair gloves, edit the scarves and hats, and find a basket for these items that fits on the shelf above the closet rod.

Jade then installs several coat hooks below the closet rod. On these hooks, she hangs scarves, umbrellas, and tote bags. Finally, she has everyone take all lightweight jackets to their rooms, with only heavy winter and dress coats remaining in the hall closet. Jade is shocked at how much space the closet now has—without her having to put in a lot of effort.

Harper

Harper is planning a complete remodel of their master closet, but she needs help. She pulls together everything necessary so she and her husband can transform the space in one weekend. Harper kicks off the project by having an electrician switch out the closet's light fixture so they can see as they work.

After pulling out all the clothes, sheets, towels, and shoes, she is amazed at how dusty the closet corners are. Harper cleans and paints the walls to refresh the space. The color is not significantly different, but now the walls are much cleaner and scuff-free.

Together, Harper and her husband install shelving units, including one with drawers. The shelves are adjustable, so Harper plays with the height until they can adequately utilize the floor space (for laundry baskets or bins with sheets in them). Once the clothing rods are up, Harper feels their closet has doubled in size.

It does not take long to fill it back up. But by placing similar items together, it's clear Harper has too many items, some of which can be donated.

WIth the brighter light, Harper also organizes her tops from black to white by color, like a rainbow. The new light allows her to see if she keeps buying similar items (mainly black tops), which she can edit down and donate. Harper feels this closet remodel is one of the most significant and important changes in her home.

Nadia

As Nadia's small kids grow into bigger clothes, she realizes their clothes work better now in closets. Her wife figures now is a good time to organize the kids' closets, so they can continue to grow into them.

The closets are not deep and have double doors with one wire rack installed. Nadia purchases two pressboard closet shelf systems that reach floor to ceiling with a single drawer in the middle.

Nadia and her wife remove the closet wire racks and install the shelves directly in the middle, since the closets have double doors. They cut apart the wire racks,so two are on one side (from the wall to the shelves), and one on the other side, for longer items. Everyday clothes make sense to keep on the lower rack, with fancier clothes on the higher rack.

Each child's room has a laundry basket under the shelves. Nadia loads shoes on the lower shelves, then odds and ends into the drawer. For now, sheets are stored on the upper shelves.

This change creates out-of-reach storage space where Nadia can wrap and put away keepsakes she doesn't want to get damaged. Using the two shelf assemblies, she and her wife have created a closet shelving system that makes sense for their now-older kids.

Takeaway

Storage spaces sometimes don't actually work well for... well, storage. Taking another (possibly non-traditional) look at these spaces may double your storage capabilities and help you find what you need.

What's one small step you can take today?

10

Paperless Organization

The Challenge

There is too much paper in my house, and I can't find the essential things when I want or even need to. This inability to pinpoint documents leaves me feeling chaotic and reactive to requests, which is stressful.

Nadia's Story

I know I'm not organized, but I don't think it has ever stopped me from getting things done. However, I fully break out into a sweat when my wife asks about a document or form or anything remotely "administrative" about our life. Our little "formal" dining room has become a dumping ground of mail, school forms, bills, and other piles. I am fine simply walking by and ignoring it, except when I can't.

We are kicking around the idea of getting pre-qualified for our next home. I realize I have no idea where our last three years of printed tax returns are, not to mention our homeowner's insurance policy. Not knowing where our documents are in our home is scary. We might have to scramble to get our information together for our pre-qualification, and it's my fault.

Personal documentation is not my only problem. With our oldest daughter in elementary school, it seems the entire house is papered with her "artistic efforts." How do teachers come up with so many crafts? Don't they all indicate stages of her development? Aren't they treasures to keep? Some days I feel we are drowning in a sea of paper. I keep thinking it would be better once we move and have more room. But will it? Will the sea just morph into an ocean?

Taking Action

To feel afloat, try "going paperless." The key to this movement? A great document scanner. There is no way around this; the better the scanner, the faster and easier this conversion becomes. It must be easy and reliable to implement.

Scanning Paper Away

Scanning: You will want a document scanner that can be set up to scan front and back. Scanning both sides may make the file size slightly larger. If there is no content on the backs, you may want to delete the blank pages in the file. But for general archiving, the default settings should be fine.

File Type: PDF file format is a universal file type for paper documents (it is not suggested to use PDFs for photographs). Most computers and phones come with a PDF reader, so this universal file type can fit almost every need.

Storage: In addition to keeping things on your hard drive, consider investing in an external backup hard drive just for your documents. Keep it simple, with a solid-state hard drive (which means there are no physical wheels spinning inside the drive that could go bad over time) and a case for portability. A 1TB drive with a case can cost less than $100 and include a warranty to help salvage the data if anything ever goes wrong. The drive could hold upwards of a million small file-size documents! It's a small investment to declutter your space and much easier to transport.

Strategy: In this no-paper movement, think about where you can take advantage of paperless services. Your bank and credit card statements are online—no need to keep a copy. Schools also keep grade cards and calendars online. The one deviation to this is tax records. Supporting printed receipts and documentation should be kept, even if they're not immediately accessible.

Emergency Binder

There is one exception to the "no-paper movement," which is an Emergency Binder. Similar to scanning and going paperless, the up-front work to create this one-stop reference guide takes a little time. However, once finished, you will only complete a quick annual update to keep the binder current. Documents should be placed in plastic sleeves for protection.

What's in this binder? Paper copies or duplicates of the following documents with divider tabs.

Identity Information

- Driver's licenses
- Passports
- Social Security cards
- Citizenship or naturalization papers
- Birth certificates
- Current work visas

Taxes

Note these are for the previous three years (with the supporting receipts and documentation saved elsewhere).

- Federal
- State
- Local
- All W2s, I9s, 1099s, and/or other documents

Insurance Policies

- Auto (and other vehicles)
- Home(s)
- Life
- Disability
- Long-term care

Banking

- End-of-year bank and credit card statement summary or screenshot from online bank system
- Each credit card (front and back with contact phone number visible)
- Mortgage statement
- Any bank or college loans
- Bond certificates or stocks
- Investments/retirement account information (end-of-year summary report is enough)
- List of all bankers and financial advisors

Medical Records

- Medical insurance cards (medical, dental, vision)
- List of all doctors and pharmacies
- List of all current medications with dosage info
- Vaccination cards or records

Other

- Latest Social Security reports (mailed or printed from the Social Security website)
- Home information (deeds, property tax assessments, builder floor plan)
- Vehicle(s) titles and registrations
- Appraisals of anything currently insured or of value
- Credit reports

- Utility account statements (just one representative copy with maybe a sticky note for login information)

An additional binder might be needed for

- Living will (instructions to family when incapacitated)
- Will (instructions to family upon death)
- Power of attorney(s)
- Trust documents
- Funeral information

Whether it is financial planning meetings, tax references, applying for credit, or simply checking on a record, this binder can make a world of difference.

You can then replicate the binder on your external hard drive. Again, a one-time setup effort to scan documents or pull PDFs from websites pays off: It's now easy and quick to access information or forward it to the insurance agent or financial planner.

Creating a "quick access folder" of identification cards and common documents can also speed up uploading processes for government or medical offices as well as other needs. This should include:

- Driver's licenses
- Passports
- Social Security cards
- Citizenship or naturalization papers
- Birth certificates
- Current work visas

- Medical insurance cards (medical, dental, vision)
- List of all current medications with dosage info
- Vaccination cards or records

Put a reminder on your calendar to review and update all paperwork and statements at the start of a new year, replacing anything outdated.

Children's Artwork

The artwork. Anyone with an elementary-age child in their lives can relate; the artwork is everywhere! Tackling the sea of crafts is a project that will allow everyone to enjoy new pieces, but not be overwhelmed by the growing piles brought home daily.

First, as everything comes home after school, ask your child what items they are most proud of. Did this hand outline of a turkey give them a sense of satisfaction, or could they not care less? Use their answers (plus your personal reaction) to filter down the mass.

Second, once filtered down, capture them digitally. If it is a certificate or art on a piece of paper, use the document scanner. If it is an art project or other three-dimensional item, take a picture with your cell phone camera using a solid backdrop like a plain wall, table, or even the floor.

Third, display those important pieces in a designated spot in the house, so everyone can enjoy them. Rotate them monthly, seasonally, and year after year by taking down the older works and repeating the cycle.

As long as you have a digital copy, you can choose to keep only essential pieces (or nothing) after your child has lost interest. As an adult, they will not want bins and bins of this material given to them.

Ways to Get Started

What struggle causes the most heartburn in your life? Is it the piles of paper lying around, not being able to find your taxes, or children's artwork swallowing the refrigerator? We all have different pain points, but the journey to relief can start with one small step.

Camryn

Camryn uses a document scanner at work, but never thought about using one at home. She purchases a scanner, and after some rearranging, places it immediately next to her computer, even closer than her printer, as a subtle hint. She works through eliminating her drawer of paper files, including maintenance records, receipts for apartment repairs, certifications, reference letters, copies of checkups and shot records for the girls, and more.

Camryn also feels a shredder is essential to dispose of these paper documents, so she tucks one under her desk. Once a month, her youngest daughter's chore is shredding everything in the "to shred" box.

Camryn feels much lighter without the heavy responsibility of printed files in a file cabinet. She experiences even more relief with the small hard drive she uses for storage, and a backup she gave her parents to hold on to. Camryn is confident that in an emergency, she will have everything she needs.

Jade

Jade realizes their family printer is also a scanner, but she never uses that part. Because it is a little older, she can only scan one side at a time. Jade decides that to prioritize what to scan, she needs to set up their Emergency Binder first.

Jade is a little overwhelmed at gathering and scanning all the information, so she enlists an accountability buddy. Her girlfriend commits to creating the same binder, and every week they agree on a section to target. Jade is shocked that within two months her binder is fully assembled. Instead of a standard black or white binder, Jade selects a bright orange one to stand out.

When finished, Jade reviews the binder with her husband, so he knows what it contains and where it is located. Flipping through it, he thinks of a few additional items to add, using plastic sheet covers to preserve them. This one binder becomes the central source of their personal information.

Harper

Harper doesn't know which is more significant: the paper files for her own family, or the mail and medical paperwork she accumulates for her parents. It seems she is always out of file cabinet space, and she does not want any more cabinets added to their small home office.

Harper decides the most pressing need is to create a binder (along with electronic backup) of her and her husband's wills and powers of attorney. Harper is surprised at the relief she feels having these secured (and giving her siblings copies).

This builds her determination to start the next step: tackling her parents' paper files. Harper lists the types of documents she will be looking for, including medical records. She uses several boxes, lined up under her desk, into which she quickly tosses the appropriate papers. After everything is sorted, she can remove all her parents' folders crowding her file cabinets.

Once a week, Harper tackles a box. She visually scans the document for date and relevance (and whether it is a duplicate). In no time, she has her boxes sorted down to the papers of importance. Harper isn't sure if she wants these files digitized or simply filed away again in a more orderly fashion, but she is delighted to reduce so much paperwork. Harper knows she can do the same with her own family files.

 Nadia

Nadia has to take some baby steps, tackling the dining room as the paper piles seem out of control. Just like sorting out a closet, she uses three bins to capture similar items and eliminate anything unnecessary. She clearly labels the bins "to keep," "binder," and "artwork."

Nadia and her wife review the artwork and make three subpiles: keep paper copy and digitize, digitize only, throw away. Nadia's wife borrows her brother's scanner. Nadia does not enjoy this task, but her wife appreciates the effort and decides to take on scanning herself. Quickly, the art pile is gone, with only a few pieces tacked up on the walls to enjoy.

It now seems easier to do the same with their remaining two bins. They agree that when the project is completely done, their reward will be a nice dinner out!

Takeaway

Taking steps to organize paperwork and implement a paperless structure can be daunting. However, the amount of work you put in can equal the amount of relief you will feel.

What's one small step you can take today?

11

Remembering Vacations

The Challenge

I invest significant time and money into creating a vacation experience for my family, but the events are fleeting. I want to carry the joy and wonder of our trips into our daily lives.

Camryn's Story

I'm looking to liven up my home office nook. Like the rest of my apartment, I haven't done much to reflect my style, let alone make it a pleasant place to work. When working from home, I am off the hook with making it look "corporate," since no clients or customers meet me here. It just has to look okay on video meetings. But looking around my bare walls, I realize my office cannot spark inspiration.

I love dreaming of what I think of as my "geographical home," which is the beach. My goal is to retire on a tropical coast one day. I relish any beach trips we take as a family, as well as the memories of more exotic beaches I visited in college. I always have a wall calendar of beautiful beaches, but nothing else in my little office speaks to me. Without visual inspiration, it makes my workday feel routine and mundane, which drains me of energy. I don't like this feeling.

Taking Action

Trinkets and items from vacations so often end up in a storage box. Everyone wants to keep these little treasures that inspire memories, but they often end up tucked away. By pulling together these pieces and getting creative, these same little treasures can be a beautiful way to remember and inspire dreams every day.

A Little Bit of Vacation

For families that often travel or visit a particular place annually, it is wonderful to focus on something little that can be brought back to form a collection. You can search online to find ideas that resonate:

- Small jelly jars and lids to collect sand from various beaches
- Keychains from each location
- Display of various coins from different countries
- Photo-montage posters from pictures taken on vacations
- Charms for a necklace or bracelet
- Braided or leather string bracelets
- Local wine, beer or other beverage bottles

Picking something to consistently keep an eye out for adds a bit of a "treasure hunt" aspect to traveling. Bringing something home to compile with similar items helps illustrate the unique culture and style of different locations. There are various ways to decorate or accessorize a room, so these items can remain present and provide pleasant reminders of a trip.

Vacation Details

When it comes to remembering a great vacation, ignore those overpriced gift shops, and don't stuff your suitcase with expensive photo books. Instead, take advantage of fabulous sales back home. Check out clearance sales at local bookstores and libraries for books reflecting where you have been.

Are you unhappy with the photos you took on your trip? Was it tough to capture iconic images in different locations? Search for wall calendars from those exact locations. Keep an eye out every spring; the yearly calendars are already on clearance. Do any bring back memories of places visited? Use those to jump-start your display.

Ways to Get Started

If you are an adult who has done some traveling, chances are you have trinkets and reminders of these trips tucked away somewhere. Pull everything out and look at what you've picked up. Search the internet for ideas on how to show off these items.

Camryn

Camryn feels like she is missing a daily dose of inspiration in her home office. Looking across her desk, she sees piles of papers and project folders. Nothing else provides motivation, besides the beach images on her wall calendar and laptop's home screen.

Camryn notices the extensive collection of seashells she and the girls have displayed in jars in various rooms around their apartment. Rummaging through the jars, she selects four near-perfect shells of various shapes. Camryn then brings them to her home office and places them on each project pile as old-fashioned paperweights. Now that these beautiful, natural treasures are incorporated into her day-to-day, Camryn can't help but smile.

When she tells the girls about this mission to liven up her home office, they decide to dig out various silk leis they have from parties and add them to the mix. Some are piled in a glass jar and put on the office shelf, instantly adding vibrant color. Her older daughter takes a realistic-looking lei and snips it apart. Camryn can't believe it at first, but her daughter strings some of the bunches of flowers and leaves onto clear fishing lines from their craft bin and attaches them to the ceiling over the desk.

Suddenly Camryn feels she is in a tropical destination! She loves that the girls are willing to jump in and help take advantage of what they have collected together, so Camryn can have an environment she enjoys.

Jade

One afternoon, Jade ventures into the basement and begins pulling out rubber tubs that she knows hold various vacation items from previous years. Mixed in with her children's artwork and birthday party photos, there are maps, coasters, paper money and coins from other countries, ticket stubs, mugs, brochures from museums, hotel stationery, cocktail napkins from famous restaurants, figurines from museums, and even a few "do not disturb" placards from hotels in different countries.

She gathers it all up and brings the items to the kitchen table. As she begins to spread everything out, organizing by type of item rather than vacation or country, her kids drift in and start looking over the pieces. Soon they are trading stories about memories of these trips, and Jade takes note of the items that seem to trigger the most excitement and joy.

With her favorites, she then searches the internet for display ideas. She likes the idea of a couple "shadow boxes"—picture frames with an actual box instead of a flat back where she can mount various pieces and hang the combined collection on the wall. She purchases two and gets started. Jade removes a small, useless wall shelf from the kitchen and moves it between the two shadow boxes in the upstairs hallway. Here she places some larger items, like mugs and little statues.

Stepping back, Jade is pleased with the results. However, her display still lacks a bit of color. She digs out a few scarves from a trip and drapes them across the shelf under the items, so the fabric hangs down. Jade is amazed that with a little digging at home and a quick purchase at the craft store, she can bring to light the family's vacation memories.

Harper

Harper realizes her daughter has a travel bug: The girl loves doing school projects about different countries. More and more, she hangs up pictures of famous destinations on the walls of her room.

One day Harper surprises her daughter with a pile of old maps—leftovers from Harper's childhood when her family traveled together. A couple of maps are even from when her own parents first traveled before they had Harper and her siblings. Harper kept these things along with vacation mementos in storage boxes, but thought her daughter would find them interesting.

Her daughter is fascinated with how big and colorful the maps are when she opens them. She is more familiar with GPS on her phone than these paper guides. However, she can easily spot where tourist attractions are located across famous cities. Some maps have annotations from the actual trips. Harper's daughter immediately organizes the maps into two groups: places she has traveled to and places she wants to go.

Harper helps her daughter hang the maps of where she has been on one bedroom wall. Her daughter then prints out a photo taken in each place and hangs it with the map. Soon a good portion of the wall is "wallpapered" with these memories.

Next, Harper and her daughter decide to do the same on the opposite wall, but for places her daughter wants to visit. Using pictures already hanging around her room, Harper's daughter prints a few more to overlay onto this set of maps. Her daughter has now created a dream wall she can view every day. Harper is glad she could repurpose these old maps to be enjoyed in a new way.

Nadia

Nadia's small family didn't travel much when the kids were tiny, but they are starting to take small road trips to family-oriented destinations. Nadia loves the idea of finding a small item they can consistently purchase and build a collection with purchases from every vacation.

Nadia does not want to spend a lot of money or lug home a lot of stuff, so she and her wife start brainstorming. They decide to collect magnets, which they have no trouble finding in any souvenir shop. Because the magnets are colorful and not fragile, they feel their daughter can take the lead in choosing a magnet on their upcoming trip. To jump-start their collection, Nadia finds a couple of magnets online to represent their previous vacations.

As their collection grows, these magnets end up on the side of the refrigerator, a central place where everyone sees them. Nadia finds herself looking over the magnets and reminiscing as she waits for dinner to cook. Nadia is pleased that without spending much (the most expensive was $10), these magnets quickly trigger impromptu conversations about favorite memories.

Takeaway

Travel and vacation can spur stories that last a lifetime. Small items can be incorporated into the home to keep those stories readily available and enjoyed.

What's one small step you can take today?

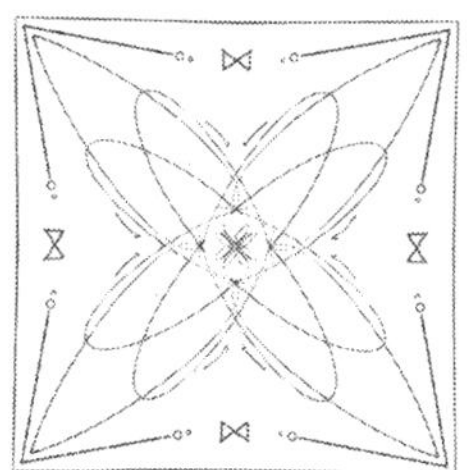

12

Power Packing for Trips

The Challenge

I love to get away, but getting ready for a trip is becoming a nightmare. Even for my kids' sleep-away camp, the packing seems to get more challenging every year. This is a repeatable process, and I'm frustrated it takes so much time.

Harper's Story

I love planning trips. It's not so much about the destination, but the planning to get there and ensuring everything goes smoothly. It's like my love language to my family.

When the kids were little, packing seemed easy and manageable. Now, I can't always plan their clothing choices for them. Sometimes the kids secretly swap out what I have packed with something less appropriate for the destination! As the kids get older, the trips seem more elaborate, with exciting destinations and extended stays. But I am beginning to dread the packing. Why is it becoming such a chore?

My children also discovered sleep-away camp in elementary school, and now have attended for several years. I love that they are comfortable staying on their own for a week, but I do not enjoy the mad dash of packing for camp. Every year the camp provides a packing list, but like a tradition, my kids seem to start from scratch, scrambling around to find everything from sleeping bags to bug spray to flashlights. Packing should not be this hard, and I'm finding it annoying.

Taking Action

An annual family vacation can be the highlight of the year, but getting ready to go can be a significant headache. A new approach to packing may be in order.

Saved Packing List

When it comes to packing up the family for vacation, the best thing to have is a saved packing list: Don't keep creating new ones. Use a spreadsheet or list-type app to develop a "master file" for vacation packing with sub-topics for different travel needs. For example, saved packing list options could include:

- General vacation (usually via air travel to a land destination with potential laundry options).
- Overnights (usually staycations a short drive away via car, laundry options not needed).
- Cruise vacation (usually five to seven days on a ship with limited laundry options).
- Cabins and camping (more outdoor considerations and limited laundry options).

These lists can also be organized by bag, which creates an instant checklist for each piece of luggage. For example, for a beach trip for a family of four, instead of throwing each person's items into their own bag (with possible duplication of items), there could be four suitcases broken out by:

- Clothes (large suitcase).
- Toiletries & pajamas (smaller suitcase or carry-on).
- Shoes and miscellaneous items (rolling duffel).
- Swim items including beach blankets and snorkel masks (rolling duffel).

Individual suitcases, by default, create an emergency bag (toiletries and pajamas) for an unexpected stop or delay, and streamline unpacking once you get to your destination. The list can also be used to pack up when leaving.

As kids get older, create a column for each person and note the number of items they need to bring (three pairs of shorts, one pair of pajamas). Print this packing list and give it to children to gather what they want to take themselves. It is still worth doing a quick once-over before they are finished, to make sure they packed the correct items. Still, it gives kids a sense of empowerment to choose what they wear, plus a sense of responsibility if they forget something (like pajamas!).

In group travel with multiple families, use a similar spreadsheet to break out who is bringing dry groceries, house supplies, or cold items (aka: who is responsible for stopping at a grocery store on the way). Start this list a month or so in advance, and keep tweaking until it is time to pack.

Pack for the Day

When going on an extended, planned trip or tour (where most days are scheduled from morning through the evening), it can help to figure out outfits for each day. This list should be specific. In a spreadsheet or list-type app, lay out each day of the trip, including where everyone is going, for how long, and if there are any restrictions. For example, touring old churches could require women to cover their arms, legs, or heads. If it is an active trip, like hiking, you'll need specific socks and boots on those days. Then plot out what clothes and shoes you'll need for each day of touring, and add in dress clothes or other changes for evening or travel.

Once laid out, look across the entire list and determine where swapping out one clothing item for something already listed can reduce the packing. This can be critical for things like shoes to reduce duplication and the weight of bags.

It's tough to pack for a family for a long trip, and it is essential to plan for the occasional backup outfit due to spills or sweat. Consider if doing laundry while traveling is an option. Taking the list on the trip and referring to it can make it easy to pull out an outfit for each day. You can also look ahead to see if weather or a change in plans will call for a particular outfit to be swapped with another day's.

Bag of Fun

A different packing challenge is taking all items you need for specific situations, like the beach, hiking, or ski trips. This travel involves gear that may be messy and shouldn't be mixed in with clothes (sand, dirt, or damp snow everywhere).

Consider investing in a rolling duffel bag that becomes the "gear bag." Select a sturdy bag on wheels with a pull handle that can be checked at the airport or strapped to the roof of a car. For example, when traveling for snorkeling, the rolling bag would contain the family's combined items:

- Masks
- Flippers
- Floating vests
- Aqua socks
- Sunscreen
- Hats

When packing for multiple people, divide each person's gear into large mesh bags within the duffel. Labeling everything, including the mesh bags, means each family member can put their items back in their own bag.

When it's time to leave, these bags return to the larger duffel. Once home, there will be sand and salt inside the bag, but that can be swept out and rinsed away. Once dry, you can properly pack everything in the bag for storage. No more scrounging around to find all the gear right before a trip. And no more trails of sand in suitcases or across the house.

Being Camp Ready

If kids are repeating an activity, like sleep-away camp every summer, consider creating a standard camp kit.

Similar to having a pre-saved travel packing list and a gear bag, having an actual camp kit can save a lot of anxiety every summer. An approved camp storage tub for each child can always contain the basics:

- Shower caddy
- Shower items
- Camp bath towels
- Swim towel
- Sheets
- Blankets
- Pillow
- Flashlight
- Bug spray
- Sunscreen
- Anything else that does not change year-to-year

When the kids return after their camp week, wash everything. Also remove batteries and check to make sure there is enough of a product to make it worth storing. If not, fall is a great time to restock sunscreen and bug spray for the following year.

Ways to Get Started

Packing for a fun trip should not be painful. Getting lists together in advance gives your brain time to process and think of anything missing. Coordinated packing can help speed up unpacking, as well as confirm nothing is left behind.

Camryn

Camryn's family is a tropical family. They prioritize taking a beach vacation once or twice a year. However, she is frustrated by the amount of gear they travel with for snorkeling, as well as everything they need to sit on the beach all day. Camryn doesn't understand why it is so difficult to find these items before every trip.

As she plans the next trip, Camryn asks the girls to go around and find everything they would take for the beach. Not only masks and fins, but also flotation jackets, beach blankets, and their usual "shell bag" for collecting shells. They pile all of it in the middle of the family room; then Camryn goes on a mission to find bags that would hold this pile. She finds one rolling bag in a closet and orders another.

Camryn isn't sure everything will fit, but she ends up with extra room in their snorkel bag for several goggles and a small tube of sunscreen. She tells the girls these are now the official "snorkel bag" and "beach bag" they will take when they travel.

Jade

Jade's two kids love to go to summer sleep-away camp. At first, they were worried about being away, but they took on the adventure quickly. Both kids go together, so it's a blast for them, as well as a mini-vacation for Jade and her husband.

Every year, Jade feels the need to rest after the mad dash of gathering everything needed for camp. What is more frustrating is she knows she already has some items, but they can't find them. Jade would not be surprised if she actually has four or more bottles of bug spray in their home, because she quickly buys what she can't find.

This year is time for a change. On the first day of summer, she has the kids list the things they always need to take, from shampoo to sunscreen to towels. Then she gives them a week to find everything in the house they should take, except their actual clothes.

Jade sets out plastic tubs, one for each kid's items. Sure enough, there are multiple bottles of bug spray and sunscreen, as well as flashlights and towels. Not only did they not have to buy supplies this year, but there's enough for the kids to pack, plus take extra to share with cabinmates.

When the kids return, instead of unpacking and putting everything away, which is how things started to disappear before, Jade washes the towels and restocks empty products. She repacks the tubs with clean towels and new supplies, and tucks the tubs out of sight until next summer, so no one takes anything out. Now she knows the kids will be ready.

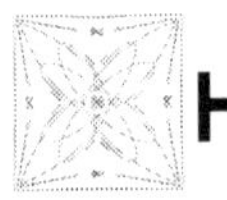

Harper

Every year Harper's family gathers for vacation at a lake house for several weeks. It is a relaxing vacation, with everyone pitching in around the house to help. Of course, before that, it is nothing but stress, as Harper feels she is the only one trying to get the family packed and out the door.

Harper decides the kids are old enough to take care of their own packing. Since they have been going to the same place for years, it is easy for Harper to make a list on the computer for each child of what to pack. She then reviews the list individually with each child, and asks them to add the things they want to bring.

She tapes the lists on the backs of their bedroom doors and notes at the bottom what day they have to be done. Once they are finished, Harper takes a quick look through each bag to ensure no one forgets anything or overpacks.

Harper cannot believe how much help it is to have each child take responsibility for their packing. She was not sure it would work, but the kids know where they are going and what to expect, so it's simple for them to pick out the right clothes. Harper's list, which indicates the number of items needed, prevented anyone from overpacking.

Harper goes back to her lists on the computer and adds the things the kids noted on their lists, so she'll have that information next year. Now she has a complete packing list for each child, ready to go every summer.

 Nadia

Nadia's extended family decides they are all taking a five-day tour of some of the beautiful cities in the southern United States. This tour will be her kids' first extended trip (not simply an overnight), and she has no idea how to not overpack. They are still relatively little, and she feels they need so much stuff for this time period.

Nadia and her wife sit down and review the itinerary. Her spouse starts a list for each day, based on what activities they are doing. On the list, under each person's name, they note what they would wear for the day, from shirt to shoes. Then, they add two additional outfits at the bottom and indicate anything extra they will need per person, including jackets and sun hats.

The list ends up being much shorter than Nadia envisioned: It will even keep them from overpacking the car. They also assemble one bag just for toys and entertainment items for the ride. No matter what they are doing each day, the bag stays in the car. Nadia feels much better about the upcoming packing and decides to keep the list to modify for future trips.

Takeaway

Travel is a great way to learn, but it shouldn't be too stressful to get ready and enjoy. Planning, as well as recruiting help, can make preparation the first step in an enjoyable vacation.

What's one small step you can take today?

13

Wedding Album 2.0

The Challenge

I had a picture-perfect wedding, but the pictures are my one regret. Overwhelmed by planning, I didn't know what I didn't know, and now I don't have a way to enjoy and preserve all the photos as I originally dreamed.

Jade's Story

With my twentieth wedding anniversary coming up, I think back on our wedding. At the time, I was so young to organize such a significant event. One of the most important aspects to me was the photographer and their photo style. I wanted images that would be timeless. I wasn't interested in video, but flipping through beautiful pictures in a luxurious album was something I knew I would treasure.

However, there were no digital images at that time. In working with the photographer, you had to select which photos went into your wedding album by watching a slideshow of the photos at the studio. After the costs of the wedding (and honeymoon!), I had miscalculated the cost of the wedding album.

I remember leaving the photographer's studio in tears. I had all the beautiful images I dreamed about, but only a fraction appeared in my album, as we couldn't afford anything more. Now, twenty years later, with so many digital capabilities available, I wonder what our album would look like if I could create it today. It makes me sad to think of what is not available for my family to enjoy.

Taking Action

If you got married in the pre-digital photo era, chances are you didn't have the opportunity to purchase or take home the entire photo collection from your wedding. What can you do? First, try to contact your wedding photographer to see if your event archive is available. To acquire the collection, it may involve purchasing the library or rights from the photographer, and scanning the prints, slides, or negatives for digital use.

Taking Another Look

Revisiting all images (not only the ones in your original album) can be an exciting event. You may discover small moments, captured initially, but forgotten with time. Reviewing what you have in your current album, for every one to two photos, you could have two to three pages expanding on the same story (rehearsal dinner, getting ready, the ceremony, departing the venue, dining, dancing, and more). Pulling a new collection of treasured images may help tell an enhanced story of your wedding.

Building a New Wedding Album

Even if you could purchase all your original prints, due to the album types at the time, you may have the photos in a magnetic (plastic page) album or a photo sleeve album. Now, online do-it-yourself websites use templates and guides to build a beautiful, high-quality wedding album. An alternative is to hire a professional to bring this album to life. They can suggest alternative album materials, bindings, and other features (like a storage box or companion book) that could be the right fit for your new, expanded album.

Ways to Get Started

Taking the time, particularly at a milestone anniversary, to rethink and maybe rebuild your original album can be something you and your spouse work on together (or even your whole family if you have children). Looking back at photos of you and all the guests can bring joy to the entire family.

Camryn

One Saturday, Camryn wakes up to find her daughters sitting on the floor with her original set of wedding photos spread all around them. At first, she is annoyed. Camryn knows the photos were in some kind of order by number, and now they are a mess. She has the loose prints, and her ex may still have the original wedding album. Even more annoying, she had put the prints away in a closet after the divorce and had no intention of looking at them again.

The girls find the photos fascinating. Like most children, they have a hard time imagining their parents as a young couple. Camryn laughs at the comments the girls are making about clothes and the age of their aunts and uncles. She starts feeling guilty that the girls want to see more of their family history.

Camryn mentions they can get the prints scanned into digital files, which the girls are used to. However, she is not interested in spending money on scanning photos of a marriage that ended. Watching her girls, Camryn realizes she has saved these slides for them, but what could the girls do with this box?

Both girls want to show their dad these photos, but Camryn doesn't know if that is a great idea. She picks up a few photos and remembers there are some wonderful group photos of each family. She had printed an enlarged group photo of the combined families and framed it after their wedding, but she got rid of that years ago. Camryn begins thinking maybe her ex-husband would like some of these family photos of himself with his parents, grandparents, and siblings. She knows that is something she will enjoy.

Camryn has the girls pick out their favorite pictures with her family, and their dad with his family. They also select some individual photos of just the bride and just the groom. A local photo shop scans the prints and delivers them on a thumb drive. Camryn and her girls then gather around the computer and use an online service to create two small books, one of Camryn and her parents, grandparents, siblings, and relatives, and one of their dad's family photo combinations. It does not take long for the books to arrive, and the girls can't wait to surprise their father with his.

Camryn enjoys working on this with the girls and remembers that the entire point of saving these photos was for them to see more of their family history. When Camryn receives a follow-up coupon from the photo book website, she orders two copies of each book to surprise the girls with their own sets at Christmas.

Jade

Jade's daughter is becoming the family historian. She constantly pulls out albums, organizes loose photos, and combines everyone's phone photos to select images from vacations, birthdays, and holidays. She's also active on the school's yearbook staff and enjoys capturing events and telling stories.

For a family history project at school, she asks Jade if she can rebuild her parents' wedding album using the same tools she is learning to use on the yearbook staff. Jade begins thinking about all the photos she does not have in her actual wedding album and wonders if that is something she can secure now. Jade reaches out to the original photographer and purchases the entire wedding photo set they have archived on slides.

Even though they are not digital, her daughter quickly begins viewing and sorting the slides to capture the full story of the wedding. Jade has those slides scanned into digital files, and her daughter says she'll do the rest.

Jade and her husband are shocked when they find a lovely photo book of their wedding sitting prominently on the same bookshelf a few weeks later. Their daughter had scanned everything, then worked with the same company that produces the yearbooks to produce this album.

As they sit with their daughter, flipping page by page, their older son joins in to look. They keep the album displayed on their shelves, and are surprised by how many visitors see it and immediately sit down to review. Jade's sisters crack jokes and tell stories of their time as bridesmaids. Jade finds it a touching treat to take a fresh look at such an important event.

Harper

While cleaning, Harper's white wedding album catches her eye. She has both the album and box of prints: something she made sure was part of the original contract with the photographer. She also has the collection of prints from disposable table cameras they provided, but she hasn't known what to do with them.

Looking at this white album in front of her, she realizes the loose prints are the only set of wedding photos she owns. There are no backups if anything happened to these tangible items.

She talks to some friends, and one recommends a local business owned by another mom. The woman scans photos in her own home. Harper likes the idea that she can keep her photos nearby, but have them turned into digital photo files. She also enjoys supporting a local entrepreneur. Harper contacts the woman and schedules to drop off the collection. It is not long before Harper receives her album and box of photos back, along with a hard drive full of every wedding photo scanned at high resolution.

When Harper plugs the drive into her computer, she finds herself engrossed in looking at the photos she has not seen in years. She can zoom in on some of the photo details, which makes it all the more fascinating. Harper decides this hard drive should go in their small fire-proof safe with essential documents and family jewelry. It is worth protecting this investment.

Nadia

Nadia's wedding anniversary is coming up, and she has no idea what to get her wife. Usually hard to buy for, Nadia wants to do something special. Searching online for ideas, she finds beautiful wedding albums. When they got married, they had not gone to the expense of creating an album. Nadia has all their photos on a DVD from the photographer, who produced a video slideshow instead. Nadia thought that was a great idea at the time, but it's not like they ever pop in the DVD to watch again.

Nadia starts checking out photo album websites, some with beautiful albums and unique photo pages. As she clicks around on one or two, Nadia quickly feels overwhelmed trying to figure out what photos to put on what pages with what templates. There are too many choices!

Nadia searches online for photo help and finds a personal photo organizer a few towns away. After talking over the phone, Nadia drops off her DVD of images and discusses preferences on the style of the album, budget, and timeframe.

A couple weeks later, Nadia receives an email from the organizer with several photo album pages attached. Nadia is thrilled: The pages are beautiful, and it's like seeing the photos again for the first time.

When it is ready, Nadia picks up her album, to avoid her wife accidentally discovering it before their anniversary. She is so eager to look at the beautiful book that she ends up sitting in her car flipping page by page. She knows this will be the perfect anniversary gift.

Takeaway

Do you have a collection of beautiful photos not getting the attention they need? Resurrecting wedding photos, whether for preservation or as a gift, can be an enjoyable activity for you or the entire family.

What's one small step you can take today?

14

SELF-CARE: Modmalas

The Challenge

I want to relax and enjoy self-care with my friends, but I'm not interested in a "spa day." I'm looking for something a bit more significant and connects me to my friends, no matter our distance.

Camryn's Story

Every year, I celebrate my birthday with my only two girlfriends, whose birthdays happen to be just days apart. This year, social distancing keeps us apart. I'm looking for a way to connect and do something more than a quarantini over Zoom. I know my friends are always game to try something new, but for me it is about the time we can spend together, even if it is virtually.

Taking Action

Nowadays, developing new social rituals can be an ongoing exploration. Connectivity is important, but not all the previous ways of spending time together make sense.

Centuries-Old Tradition Still Relevant Today

An excellent chance for women to connect is to build Modmalas together.

A mala is a string of beads (traditionally 108 for a necklace, but there are bracelet lengths) that allow you to physically keep track of your mantras (or intentions) as you meditate and sit silently or in connection with others. With a Modmala kit, friends can sit physically or virtually together and build individual mala necklaces.

Using the kit, find a small bowl to put all the beads in and have the necklace string unfolded and ready. When everyone is prepared, take some time to walk through a brief meditation (from an app or website) to center everyone's minds and hearts. This meditation allows everyone to shake off the day, relax, and be present in the gathering—whether in person or virtual.

Next, start to string the first bead and bring your intention to that bead. Tie a knot to hold that bead in place, then move to the next one. Then, (if physically together) exchange necklaces and string a bead for each other, bringing an intention to their necklace and your friendship. Exchange again until everyone has strung one bead for each other—so you can bring an intention to each friend. If virtual, everyone adds a bead to their own Modmala with a focused intention for a specific friend and relationship; then repeat for everyone in the group.

Continue to sit comfortably in a quiet space and keep your hands busy stringing and knotting as you chat. Simultaneously, continue to silently set an intention with every bead. It will feel like an old-time sewing circle—a gathering that allowed women to connect while also completing something tangible.

When you wear your mala, you know you're carrying your friends' intentions for you and your life. Modmala kits are easy to order so you can replicate the same experience with close friends anywhere.

Ways to Get Started

Completing a Modmala with friends is an intentional type of celebration. Wearing your Modmala or keeping it present in your space continues that joyous connection you have established.

Camryn

Camryn has two close girlfriends with whom she loves connecting. They live a few hours apart but make a point to schedule lunches regularly. Now that they are reluctant to gather in a public setting, Camryn wants to find an alternative with more meaning.

When she discovers the Modmala, she sends a link to her friends to explain the tradition. They are both intrigued and order their personal Modmalas. They can customize both the colors (beads and a tassel) as well as the charm that hangs at the bottom (silver or gold with a symbol holding meaning for them personally). They set up a block of time (three hours) with spouses and kids occupied elsewhere so they can talk uninterrupted.

They virtually share their specific Modmala pieces and why those pieces have meaning for them. Camryn pulls up a brief meditation on her phone app and plays it for all of them to become more present in the event. It feels awkward as they start with their beads, but they quickly form a pattern of chatting and sharing, while mentally pausing and making an intention with every bead. Camryn feels the time fly by—like an extended meditation but with a personal connection. All three agree it was a fantastic way to catch up, and now they each have a treasured item that represents their friendship.

Takeaway

Distance or time challenges can allow friends to brainstorm new ways to connect and find alternative social interactions. Even an ancient practice can fit in a modern world and bring comfort, intention, and joy to those who participate.

What's one small step you can take today?

Part 3

Your Girlfriend's Guide to Growing with Family & Friends

15

Simplifying the Big Stuff in Your Home

The Challenge

I don't feel like my house reflects my ideal home. How can I take back space in my home, currently occupied with furniture pieces that do not fit our life? Do I need to give myself permission to let go of the things in my space?

Nadia's Story

I inherited many furniture pieces from both my family and my in-laws. I guess our starter home was the place to deposit items no one could bear to let go of.

Recently, I spoke to some moms with older children. Their kids were graduating and heading out on their own. My friends wanted to scale down, but were disappointed their children didn't want any of the family's big, bulky furniture: pieces these women had saved all these years. Even as the kids started new journeys, these traditional pieces were of no interest, and didn't reflect the children's lives they were creating for themselves. Having accumulated these pieces myself, I understood both the moms' disappointment and their kids' lack of interest.

Now, as I'm walking around my own home, I'm looking with a fresh eye at these inherited furniture pieces that I usually ignore. Most of it was not my style, and much of it is in areas we barely use. Currently, they serve as a spot to pile things we don't know what to do with. Do I expect to move this furniture into a new home? Am I holding onto it for another fifteen years for my kids? Do I even want it, despite its legacy? Will I feel guilty about getting rid of it?

Taking Action

Are there unused areas of your home with furniture that doesn't belong in your lifestyle? Some items could be leftover from starting a home, some inherited, some bought on a whim. But that doesn't mean they should remain forever.

Family Furniture

Walk around and review significant items in your home: not according to sheer size, but to what they mean (or do not mean) to you. An example can be a family piano in an unused, formal living room. Upon reflection, this may feel like a "weight" rather than an item that sparks joy. It may be a reminder that no one in the family is interested in the piano, despite the investment or tradition it may represent.

The Guest Room

The guest bedroom may be another underutilized spot. It may be set up to accommodate a guest who occasionally spends the night. Over time, it morphs into a storage room with an ironing board, suitcases, and winter coats.

Think about what your family does and how you live. Do you have guests frequently enough to reserve an entire room for them? Or would the space be better utilized as a gym, small den, or office?

Could it serve as an excellent gaming room? Combine board games, video games, a TV, a table, and comfy chairs. You may find this becomes the most-used room! Creating a space of motivation and inspiration can breathe new life into a home.

Ways to Get Started

Bringing focus and design together in an area of your home can shine new light on a neglected space.

Camryn

One morning, Camryn starts looking at the upright piano taking up so much space in the corner of their family room. She desperately lobbied for it when her parents downsized, as she took piano lessons the longest. However, having held on to it for more than twelve years, she now examines the guilt-driven list of tasks that runs through her head:

- It needs to be tuned.
- The bench legs need to be tightened.
- The lamp over the sheet music needs to be replaced.
- I need to stop using it as a storage table.
- I should try to schedule lessons for myself.
- The girls have lost interest in it.

She takes a step back and recognizes the truth: her daughters do not have any interest in the piano. Camryn thinks she should take lessons herself, but does not have the time or patience to try them at this point in her life.

With this recognition and reconciliation, she suddenly feels free to offer the piano to her extended family members, where someone else might discover a wonderful gift. She becomes excited to pass the piano on to her niece and nephews and reclaim the space in her home. Her daughters said they would like that area as a centralized homework spot. Camryn thinks that sounds wonderful!

Jade

Jade and her daughter have arts and crafts materials spread all over the house, often forgotten about. As they look around again for drawing supplies, they start talking about what a treat it would be to have all their creative items in one space. Jade challenges her daughter. Could they turn the unused guest bedroom into an art room? Could this small makeover be accomplished without spending a cent?

First, they empty the guest bedroom, and Jade plans to donate the furniture. They remove the heavy, room-darkening curtains from the windows so light shines in. They set up two working spaces so they can have room to spread out.

Looking at the bedroom's large armoire with a broken drawer pull, they decide it will make a perfect storage unit, so they paint it with leftover wall paint. By changing it from dark wood to light ivory with a white interior and new pulls, the armoire takes on a new life.

Next, they gather any unused storage items like shelves, cubbies, baskets, and jars that can be used in a craft room. Then they go on a mission to collect every art and craft supply across the house. They can not believe all they discover!

Finally, after finding a proper place for everything, they do a bit of decorating. Her daughter grabs some extra holiday lights, while Jade brings in a couple of cozy rugs. Suddenly, they have an excellent craft room without spending a cent.

Jade and her daughter are both excited they could take a stale, unused room that always had the door shut, and transform it into a room full of energy and joy.

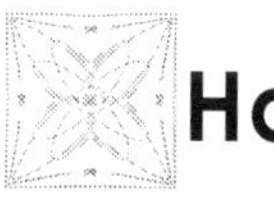

Harper

Harper is in a bind. She no longer wants the bulky dining room suit she originally inherited from her in-laws. All the furniture, cabinets, and baseboards in her home are a light shade, making the house feel bright and open.

However, this suit of furniture is dark wood with huge pieces:

- A hutch for which she has no china.
- A sideboard server which she has no room to fold out.
- A curio cabinet for which Harper does not have items to display.
- A large dining table with several leaves that she can't insert, or the table will not fit in the room.
- A set of massive dining chairs.

Although Harper's family entertains, their serving style is usually a buffet, with everyone gathering outside if it's nice. They sit in this dining room once a year at Thanksgiving. As the family grows, the room becomes tight with people and furniture.

Jade finally works up the courage to discuss the dining room furniture situation with her husband. She does not want to offend him or his family, as it was a wonderful gesture when his parents handed it off years ago. But now Harper is more annoyed by the furniture than grateful. Her husband doesn't seem too concerned about getting rid of the furniture and encourages Harper to call her mother-in-law.

Harper apologizes to her mother-in-law, saying she was grateful when they first received the furniture, but she no longer has any use (or space) for the suit. Surprisingly, her mother-in-law is not upset. She had forgotten all about the furniture and usually didn't take much notice of it at Thanksgiving. However, she mentions the local senior center always needs quality furniture.

Harper feels such a relief. She contacts the center and follows up with pictures of the furniture. Once the movers leave, Harper returns to an empty dining room and realizes there are so many possibilities to transform the room for her family.

Nadia

Nadia has a bulky traditional writing desk crammed into their guest bedroom. It was her mother's, and she feels loyalty by holding on to it. However, the guest bedroom is not an office. Nadia dislikes being tucked away from the heyday of their lives, so bills, other paperwork, her laptop, and other office items are spread out in the dining room.

Nadia's wife finds this extremely frustrating. Not only is their dining room not functioning as a dining room, but the guest bedroom is also cramped and not terribly comfortable for guests that stay over. She asks Nadia to either move the desk down to the dining room (despite lacking extra space for it) or consider getting rid of it.

Nadia is torn. She knows in her heart she will not use it. In her mind, the desk was so much her mother's that it doesn't feel like her own. Nadia sits in the guest bedroom one afternoon and meditates on the desk. Nadia looks back on the times she peeked inside the drawers as a child. She thought of the number of times she helped move the desk as her mother kept downsizing. Finally, she realizes this isn't the way Nadia wants to remember and pay tribute to her mom. Keeping a bulky piece of furniture that does not bring her joy (and actually brings anxiety to her marriage) helps Nadia make up her mind.

She clears everything off the top of the desk and ensures the drawers are empty. She gets out the wood polish and goes over it until the desk and its drawer pulls are shining. Opening the curtains and raising the blinds, Nadia takes several pictures of the desk in the sunlight. She prints the pictures and tucks them into a family album from her childhood. Then she takes the same pictures and posts them online to sell the desk.

An older gentleman quickly scoops up the treasure. His two sons said their father is excited to place this in front of a large picture window, so he can write and look outside. This makes Nadia happy that something she felt was an obligation and burden will be a sheer delight for someone else. In her heart, she knows it was the right decision.

Takeaway

In the United States, there is a cultural trend around decluttering, but it can focus on the small stuff. Don't be afraid to look at some of those big pieces you don't even know why you still have. Now is the time to refresh your home by bringing life to areas you simply walked by before. The "heavy" item that weighs you down may be someone else's uplifting joy.

What's one small step you can take today?

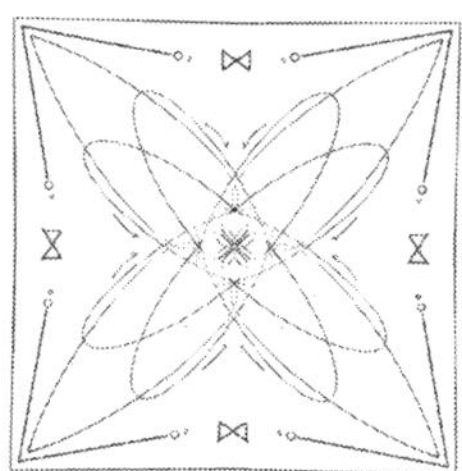

16

Family Device Management

The Challenge

I'm concerned about how much time my family spends on their devices and gaming systems. Gaming is often portrayed as a "bad" hobby, but kids love it. In addition, my kids seem to always have their smartphones in their hands. I want to have better control over these devices.

Harper's Story

My husband and I believe our children are responsible enough to have smartphones. They need to reach each other, and I like seeing their locations when they are with friends. However, it seems like they are on their phones more and more. I remember as a kid being on the house phone for hours talking to girlfriends, but smartphones are different and capable of so much more.

I hear my kids discussing nasty messages that circulate from other kids at school: messages that disappear. I wonder if the phones (or maybe certain apps) are not the best for them at this age. I am so conflicted. I want to keep them safe and protected, but I know these digital devices are part of daily living.

Taking Action

The proliferation of Wi-Fi and cellular data has liberated computer and device users: they can be anywhere and connect to just about anything. While the possibilities are endless, that wide-open frontier is not something we usually want to unleash for kids. Using both hardware and software safeguards can help.

Understanding Technology Language

To do more than use a cell phone, some items and terms need to become familiar.

Wireless router: Used to provide access to the internet or a private computer network

Access point: A hardware device that allows wireless-capable devices and wired networks to connect through a wireless standard, including Wi-Fi or Bluetooth

VPN (Virtual Private Network): A feature that allows the user to bypass any local network security measures, usually by rerouting your network traffic to another router on the internet. During your periodic checks of your child's device, look for a "VPN" symbol in the menu bar when surfing.

MAC address: A unique "digital fingerprint" ID number assigned to each device with a connection to the internet. This address is represented as a string of numbers in pairs of two, separated by a semicolon or dashes (12:34:56:78:90). This address will allow you to precisely control that device using its ID (this does not refer to a Mac versus PC system).

Bringing Wi-Fi Into the Home

Typically, a residential internet provider can install their specific Wi-Fi router. Combining a wireless router with access point functionality can cover an entire house, so there are no dead zones. The router also has key features you can leverage to regulate your child's internet usage:

Password settings: Secure your Wi-Fi access with a password, and change the default password on your router to something not easily revealed (not a birthday or specific name).

Time settings: Control when the internet is available by the time of day. For example, the home office computer may be connected to the internet all the time (but is password-protected from the kids). However, kids' laptops may lose connectivity at 9:00 p.m.

Website filter settings: Control any websites the kids are prohibited from visiting until a certain age. For example, they may not reach YouTube or Netflix from their device until you deem them old enough.

Reporting: Many routers come with a website you can use to see where your kids are surfing. This ability to see browsing history can be used less to "penalize" and more to prompt conversation. What were you looking for on this website? Is there something you don't understand?

Most manufacturers now include a "parental controls" section in the router management menu. Each manufacturer does it differently, and it may take a bit of tweaking to make the settings work for your family. Once the router works, enable parental controls, and use the MAC address of the device to control specific access. Test it with a single device to make sure it is working, then change the MAC address for the devices with limitations. Rules can also be added to disable a device, like if you need to disable a gaming system's connectivity for a weekend as a penalty.

Note many smart devices, like phones, will "call home" to their operating system's respective servers during overnight hours to run updates. If blocking these devices at bedtime, consider unblocking them from 1:00 a.m. to 4:00 a.m. If the device can't reach its server through Wi-Fi, it might attempt the connection via your cellular network, which can run up your data usage in the overnight hours.

It is challenging to stop smart kids from working around these settings, as they share things like Wi-Fi passwords with neighbors. They will also try to hop connectivity points and talk to their friends about VPN apps. Remember, managing your child's devices is crucial as they grow and mature. However, these steps can reduce wayward surfing and help you introduce and guide kids through the world wide web.

Smartphone Ownership

One of the biggest challenges with devices is introducing smartphones and tablets to kids. The information out there can be conflicting. Many studies state that young children learn even faster with a tablet or smart device; however, the impact of social media on children can be negative. How to draw the line?

As a parent, a critical approach is to realize that smartphones and tablets are adult tools that you allow your children to use. The technology belongs to you, the adult, and this should be clear to your children. As the adult, you will:

- Review everything on the phone. This includes apps, texts, messaging systems, and photos. This review must be frequent, and feel free to take the device at any time to review.

- Remove the device at night. Having children turn in all devices at bedtime promotes sleep. A kid's phone will continue to buzz with group text messages well after midnight despite your steps, so remove it and power it off. Kids will turn to the device for stimulation and forgo rest if they have the opportunity.

- Talk about the devices. Reviewing the device and asking about specific chats help a parent understand social situations at school. This may be something the child is directly involved in, or witnessing a friend go through. These are great opportunities to support your child and have critical conversations.

- Stay informed about technology. Keep a watchful eye on the latest apps and ways kids are trying to circumvent controls. Schools, government programs, and the media continually provide avenues to learn more.

- Take control of the device. Parents can restrict many features on cell phones and tablets, including the ability to:

    - Add apps.

    - Change the primary account information.

    - Turn off phone tracking.

    - Run on a cellular network (restricting use only to Wi-Fi).

    - Add people to multiplayer games.
    - Make purchases within apps or games.

- Back up the devices. Regularly back up all devices to a central computer at home, in addition to the cloud.

Controlling Those Apps

Plenty of games and applications could be of concern for parents or school administrators. These applications may allow kids to post nasty anonymous comments about classmates. This type of messaging is one of many forms of cyberbullying.

Introducing a social application is more than just installing it on a device. It is essential to have a conversation with your child.

- Why is this app important?
- How are your friends using it?
- Do you understand the risks or negative impacts of this app?

A new app that "everyone has" may not be the best or safest for a child. Check out the specifics of the app for yourself and search for articles or blogs written about that app.

Certain apps may not be appropriate at certain ages, and parents will have to revisit the question later down the line. The key is to determine if benefits outweigh risks. More importantly, creating the opportunity to talk with children about these choices is the most significant technology lesson of all.

Having a Bit of Technology Fun

Teenagers don't seem to realize hours go by when immersed in their smartphone or tablet. They may be chatting and having a fun conversation, but it is easy to lose the day.

Periodically reviewing kids' texts helps parents understand the dynamics and health of childhood friendships. These relationships can alter dramatically, and it is essential to keep children grounded in what friendship means.

An unfortunate realization when reviewing this content is seeing the language kids use with their peers, which may not usually come out of their mouths at home. Teenagers desperately try to appear more mature by using every four-letter word they can think of, but it makes for some pretty inane text conversation.

Something fun for parents is utilizing the "autocorrect" feature of a phone, so typing in those four-letter words becomes impossible. Through this tool, you can halt certain words: b*#ch becomes "blaze-smoldering poo pile" and f*#k becomes "flugelhorn."

Kids become more aware of their language when it is constantly swapped for something nonsensical. For parents, it makes reviewing these online conversations a bit more humorous.

Ways to Get Started

Technology is a big responsibility for both parents and their children. There are teachable moments through this journey, but it takes attention to guide them safely.

Camryn

Camryn feels the girls are handling their phones well for their ages, but as they get more comfortable with their devices, she sees they are adding applications she disapproves of. She decides to add password controls for their phones, so they have to ask for a new app.

Camryn may do some homework, including researching the app and talking to other moms. She sets the expectation that adding an app is not a given. For certain social media apps, Camryn feels it is important to discuss their usage with her girls, as well as warning signs about friends' behavior within the app.

Camryn knows they can't live without their mobile connection. It is frustrating there is so much to continuously learn, but their safety keeps her motivated.

Jade

Jade and her husband are considering getting a faster level of internet service for their home. With more devices and streaming opportunities, it makes sense. The upgrade comes with a new router and wireless access point to be installed by the provider.

Once installed, Jade and her husband work with the technician to set up access passwords and learn more about setting controls for specific devices' internet access. It is a lot to learn, but they quickly adapt to managing these functions. They also realize these are not universal settings. Different access levels or times available are granted based on the kids' ages.

Jade's husband takes a genuine interest in technology and continues to research and learn more about managing access. He and Jade talk over concerns and possible changes as they become more comfortable. Discussing this technology with other parents is also a chance to share what they have set up and learn ideas other parents use.

Harper

Harper is surprised when the school begins asking children to bring phones to class for research. It is a significant responsibility, and providing a gradual approach to using devices makes sense.

As Harper and her husband develop rules for mobile phones, she is adamant they collect cell phones at night. She prioritizes sleep for her kids and knows parents who worry when their kids are text messaging throughout the night. Harper's children resist the phone collection, but Harper and her husband present a united front on this point.

They set up a charging station in their bedroom at the furthest corner from their door. As Harper says good night, she collects the phones and plugs them all in to charge overnight. In addition, she sometimes scrolls through their messages and apps to monitor for potential problems. Over time, this process becomes such a regular occurrence that her kids get used to it.

Nadia

Nadia is not looking forward to her kids being old enough for cell phones, but she knows that even at a young age, her daughter is quickly learning to love digital tablets. Nadia feels it is important to start managing her daughter's use early to set expectations as she grows.

Nadia makes a big deal about granting "tablet time" and usually ties it to some accomplishments or other indicators that her daughter earned this time. Nadia demonstrates the tablet has a timer for use. When the time is up, her daughter "tucks the tablet in bed" inside a cabinet where it can charge.

Because of this expectation, her daughter often does not resist when time is up. Nadia also ensures that when her daughter is finished, there is something else to do, so her daughter can see the tablet as just another option for play during their day.

Takeaway

It is difficult to consider living without devices, but it doesn't mean access and use is a free-for-all. Parents have every right to create boundaries and set expectations with their children, which provides important lessons.

What's one small step you can take today?

17

Financial Teachable Moments

The Challenge

I want to teach my kids to work hard and earn money, but using an allowance with a cash payment does not work in our lives. Once they earn their money, I want to demonstrate better approaches to spending before they move out on their own.

 Jade's Story

The kids are in that in-between stage where they can't get a job or earn much money, but they certainly want to spend it. They meet friends after football games for a late meal, they head to the mall on Saturdays, and they always seem to need to fill up the car. I could extend their list of chores so they could earn more allowance. That could help me out too.

However, I struggle to remember to get cash to pay them. I don't even remember to pay them week over week. It then blows up into a big deal when the kids realize they haven't been paid or are back to asking for money (which, of course, I don't have the cash for). This traditional allowance model is just not working. Do families even do this anymore, or am I just lousy at this? I feel like I should be providing some kind of lesson in money management, but how can I teach it when I can barely manage it myself?

Taking Action

Teaching spending and savings lessons, paired with creative ways of engaging kids with money, builds healthy fiscal habits.

Allowance as a Variety of Life Lessons

One way to handle allowance is splitting the monthly amount and giving it to them twice a month, like adults get paid. The kids then have to manage paycheck to paycheck.

Depending on the age, kids can have a bank account at the same bank as their parents. This new account means their allowance can be a quick online bank transfer at the end of the pay period. This can be automated, so parents no longer forget to get cash. Another option is Venmo or other cash payment apps, depending on the child's age.

For tweens and early teens, there are apps like Greenlight, which provide the child with a prepaid card, with the parent controlling when and how much money is loaded on. The app can list all chores to be completed, and make their allowance payment contingent on checklist completion. This too can be automated, but parents can approve or pause the payment.

To make this shift, it can take some discussion and planning. First, revisit the list of designated chores for the month, with some chores being weekly. Post the list on the refrigerator for visibility, text it to the kids, or use a phone app that creates shared lists. At the end of the week, the kids must turn in their completed chore list via marking on the poster, texting a confirmation, or checking off the tasks in the app. That action determines if they receive an entire paycheck.

Second, negotiate a fixed amount based roughly on what they initially received as a weekly cash allowance. Also, determine the dollar amount penalty for them not completing their chores.

Third, outline with the kids what the allowance means in terms of spending. Which types of expenditures are they now responsible for versus what spending parents will cover? For example, they may meet friends for food or shopping, in which case money spent comes out of their allowance. School clothes and groceries do not.

Making Good Buying Decisions

If your child enjoys shopping locally or online for clothes, a great way to introduce smart buying to kids is through a subscription-based clothing site. These sites help you save time and money:

- No driving to the mall
- Compare items to what is already in your closet

- Stop and review the cost (rather than impulse purchasing)
- Returns are as easy as bagging up the items and popping them into the mailbox

Teens in particular can benefit from a subscription clothing service, as they move into junior and adult clothing sizes. They provide the opportunity to try new items, yet still create their distinctive style. These services also establish a regular shopping frequency, and help them learn how to make more "educated". purchases.

The reality is when kids are at the mall with friends, parents never know what clothing will come home with them, or if it is redundant to pieces they already own. Kids (like adults) can be shopping blindly and without purpose, but parents can bring more education and structure to their shopping habits.

Ways to Get Started

It is essential to talk about the potential challenges associated with setting up an allowance system. Everyone should expect kids to make mistakes in managing their money and making wise purchases. But at least the mistakes are happening now, rather than in college where they could rack up credit card debt, or as an adult where they may only afford to pay their rent and not live. Parents can watch their children learn and build their money management skills.

Camryn

Camryn thinks this is a good time to introduce her older daughter to a subscription-based clothing company. Camryn's goal is to teach her daughter how to make intelligent purchases without overextending herself. They discuss the frequency of ordering a box based on her daughter consistently completing her chores and contributing to the subscription.

After looking around online, they decide on a company that fits her daughter's style. In the subscription account registration, they set limits on different clothing items so her daughter will not be tempted to overspend. They also set up the frequency of purchases, staggering deliveries to fit within their overall budget (quarterly rather than monthly). Finally, they agree that for every item her daughter purchases, one item must come out of her closet for donation.

On the subscription site, Camryn's daughter communicates with an assigned stylist through messages and online photo boards, so the stylist can get to know her tastes. With every box delivered, Camryn's daughter experiences the joy of opening something new and trying on fun pieces she may never have found locally. However, she also has time to think through each item and whether it makes sense to add to her closet. She compares the items she receives to what she already has, and whether a piece is a one-time impulse or more of an investment.

Camryn believes it's beneficial for her daughter to have time to pause and compare before making a final purchase. She's hopeful she can learn some positive shopping habits, be mindful in managing her spending, and still have some fun!

 Jade

Since Jade's children already have bank accounts, she decides they could go to a "direct deposit" allowance mode, with payments made every two weeks. It would model what they would experience when they do have jobs. With this plan, she mentions there will be no extra transfers to cover any shortage in their accounts.

She assumed they would be thrilled to receive a lump sum twice a month, larger than one week's allowance. Her son is happy with the plan at first. Quickly he realizes he needs reminders for himself that if he is saving for something, he can't just spend it when he sees that money arrive.

In contrast, her daughter is anxious about the payments. She is nervous about whether she can manage her money across the month. Jade realizes both reactions are a good sign. She is challenging her kids to manage money like adults: what great skills to build.

The first month is fascinating to watch. Jade's daughter doesn't make it through without going broke, but she improves in her second month. Her son struggles with not agreeing to in-app purchases. He also quickly realizes gaming upgrades at $1 or $2 a day start to add up, and he's struggling to save. Jade sometimes has to remind the kids certain things they want now will come out of their pockets, not hers.

Despite wanting him to save, Jade is pleased to see her son buy several neighborhood kids desserts from the ice cream truck, because he can. The driver gives her son an extra treat for being so generous. Managing his own money brings a sense of empowerment and generosity, which are great lessons.

Harper

Harper keeps a chore list on the side of the refrigerator. Even though her older children now think this is lame, Harper likes the visual reminder. But she realizes she is not updating the chores as the kids get older. She also never considers reducing their allowance if they choose not to do a chore.

Over dinner, the family discusses the chore list. Harper considers activities the kids are now old enough to take on, and that she and her husband have always done. Harper lists these new chores, including washing the sheets and towels, mowing the lawn, and cleaning up the dog waste. Extra tasks can justify a higher allowance, but also a higher penalty if they skip the chore.

The kids negotiate the value of each chore. At first, Harper thinks it is strange to put a price on each task, but knowing she could itemize and deduct for duties not completed makes sense. Life is easier when she can remind her teenagers they are losing money out of their own pockets if they don't finish their chores.

 Nadia

Nadia recognizes that her oldest daughter can start completing basic chores. She and her wife discuss what chores they think their first grader could complete, but agree money isn't the right incentive at this age. They decide to match all three assigned chores with an extension to her limited device time. Their daughter can earn an extra five minutes for every chore she finishes.

Their daughter first needs reinforcement to understand. Once it clicks, she latches on to the idea of being a helper and receiving something fun as a result. In the summer, they change the payment to "extra time outside" or even a one-on-one walk around the block with one of them (no baby brother included). Nadia likes how her daughter understands that working hard brings rewards.

Takeaway

There are many opportunities to teach kids not only about working hard to earn money, but also about spending it wisely. Whether it be stretching their income over several weeks or slowing down and analyzing a purchase, the lessons are valuable and can start early. What they may find irritating now, they will be grateful for later in life.

What's one small step you can take today?

18

Want Versus Need Lessons

The Challenge

One of the most challenging things to learn in life is to want versus need. In an age of one-click ordering, how can I help my kids understand the difference when I know I am not setting the best example?

Camryn's Story

I raised my girls to be more excited by experiences than things. It's in my nature to learn more about the world at any opportunity, and I share that with them. We have enjoyed so many adventures and traveled extensively, while only keeping little mementos from these trips.

But now in middle school, it seems like they suddenly ask for things all the time. Every time I turn around, one wants to go shopping, and the other requests to order something. I try to make them accountable, having to buy some things with their own allowance, but I'm worried. Are they becoming materialistic? What can I do to stop that trend, or is it too late? This constant asking for things goes against everything I value, and I find this frustrating.

Taking Action

Want versus need is a question with which everyone wrestles. A want focuses on your desire to have something (or do something). A need is when something is essential. At the core are the words desire versus essential.

When looking to rein in spending or build financial integrity, past purchases can be examined as want versus need. The goal is to curtail purchasing items in the want category, which can be causing financial issues like credit card debt.

As children evolve into their ability to spend, helping them distinguish this difference early can save them years of financial distress. Establishing clear rules around allowances, when children should pay for their own items, and consequences for overspending are all methods for teaching.

In addition, simplistic examples in your own life can help drive home the point. If everyone is tired and asking for fast food on the way home (rather than making a meal), asking if that fast food stop is worth not doing something planned for the weekend, or giving to a cause they had discussed, spotlights the want versus need choice.

Ways to Get Started

It can be challenging to teach lessons about want versus need, especially if this is also a struggle as an adult. Teaming up with your kids to practice the same strategies can help the entire household and its finances.

Camryn

Camryn is tired of her girls constantly asking for stuff. Whether it is peer pressure at school, influencers on social media, or advertising everywhere, the girls act like they never have enough. Camryn tries to toe the line on controlling their spending. However, in weak moments, particularly when she is tired, she has been known to give in, especially for something that takes one click to order and will arrive within the week.

Out of frustration, Camryn decides to make their behavior more visible to the girls. She knows they have no idea how many times they ask or discuss things to purchase. She develops a strategy of putting two pieces of paper on the fridge, one for each daughter with their name at the top. She divides the paper into two columns; the left is titled "Want," and the title on the right is "Need." For each girl, she jots down recent wants they have expressed. The need column is blank (since Camryn, of course, takes care of their essential needs).

She then shows the girls the lists. Every time they come to Camryn to ask for something, they have to write it down. If, out of habit, they do ask, Camryn will redirect them to the lists. They need to determine where each item they are asking for belongs.

On Sundays, the three of them will review the sheets and determine if items are in the correct columns. Once they finish their analysis, Camryn will discuss with each daughter whether there's something they truly need on the list—or which one item is truly important from the "want" side.

The girls start completing their want lists like a list for Santa. If they start to ask for something in conversation, Camryn reminds them to "go put it on the list." By Sunday as they review, both girls are embarrassed at how long their lists are, particularly since almost all of it falls in the "want" column. They note some needs, and Camryn discusses each one by asking how necessary each item is.

Ultimately, upon reflection, the girls scratch out most of the "want" items. They have lost interest, or something else now seems more important. In some cases, the girls do not even remember saying they wanted something.

This ongoing activity is eye-opening for all three of them, and over time their want columns become shorter and shorter. Camryn is proud the girls are beginning to understand this fundamental difference, and notes a few things to make her Christmas shopping a lot easier!

Jade

In Jade's ongoing quest to reduce the amount of stuff in their house—while reducing the number of times she goes shopping—she becomes acutely aware of how much the kids have. There are old presents they no longer care about, plus tons of activity equipment they have outgrown or no longer need. It seems like their house holds so much of the past, yet everyone has lost interest.

This doesn't stop the kids from wanting something else or trying something new. She appreciates their sense of adventure and being open-minded about trying new things, but she begins to resent the extra rounds of purchasing.

Jade and her husband frequently talk about the lack of space and the messes in closets and storage areas. They decide the best thing is to flip the approach. If her kids want to try something new or need new stuff for their hobby or sport, they have to give back first. There will be no shopping trip unless there's a giving trip.

As her son needs all new gear for his summer camps, Jade insists he finds all his old gear, clean it, and donate it to a children's organization or charity. Only when all the gear is gone will Jade entertain purchasing new equipment. The same holds true for her daughter. Even for hobbies like crafts, her daughter has to reuse what she has or donate what she no longer needs before buying something new.

Jade notices her kids feel good about gathering up items. Taking the time to clean, refresh, and donate things feels better than tossing them out. As their needs evolve, Jade notices old items leaving.

Harper

Harper wrestles with her children expecting what they want to magically appear when they want it. Her work ethic around earning what you want conflicts with giving in to their every desire. Harper wants to instill an understanding of working hard to earn new things.

Harper can easily list key things her kids always ask for. She decides to demonstrate a transactional approach to earn what they want. She turns her kids' chore list into a bartering list. For example, if her daughter wants another pair of shoes because they are in fashion, then two weeks' worth of chores equals that new pair of shoes (instead of an allowance). Seven chores equals one small piece of sports equipment for either of her sons.

Her kids begin to think more about what they can do to earn something, rather than simply asking for it. They try to negotiate with Harper to determine how to earn an item. Sometimes Harper makes it challenging, particularly for things she feels may be fleeting interests, and not something they care about long-term. Sometimes, the kids realize the work effort isn't worth their desired item. She also sees her kids stay laser-focused on getting the work done to earn something they want.

Harper appreciates her kids are trying to negotiate better terms (not that they always succeed). Household chores have become a fun way to learn many new and essential skills!

Nadia

Nadia's daughter is caught up in an endless cycle of birthday parties for her classmates. It seems like every other weekend there is another party. There are two things Nadia finds frustrating about these events. First, this forces them to constantly be shopping for a gift, which means her daughter often takes home something as well. Second, her daughter returns home from a party with a bag full of "treats," usually cheap, disposable plastic toys with no significance. The entire hamster wheel seems like a lesson in materialism.

Nadia decides to take control of the situation. First, she begins prepping her daughter for their birthday gift shopping trips. Nadia frequently repeats they are in the store to buy one, and only one, item: the birthday gift. Even if it is easier for Nadia to pick up a few personal things while in the store, she holds back. Her daughter learns that no matter how many times she asks for something she passes in an aisle, they are leaving with only one item. At first, these trips are tough. Nadia recognizes the cues her daughter has established to try to get what she wants. On a rough day, it takes all of Nadia's energy to say no. But the "one item" rule makes it a bit easier.

The second thing Nadia does is clamp down on the "gift bags" coming from parties. She had no idea when and how this trend started, with the birthday family giving everyone who attends a gift. It seems ridiculous and a waste of money. When Nadia

RSVPs to a party, she clearly lets the mom know her daughter is simply there to celebrate the birthday, and she prefers her daughter not receive anything in return.

As Nadia sends these messages, a few moms reach out asking about her RSVP note, trying to understand the intention. One of Nadia's closer mom friends is so struck by the request that she decides to scrap the gift bags she intended to provide at her child's party. Instead, the mom and her daughter make brownies and package one for each child to take home (for themselves or their moms), but does not provide anything else.

Several moms comment that skipping the requisite gift bag expectation is a relief: one less thing to tackle while prepping for a small child's birthday party. Nadia isn't sure if her daughter will pick up on these lessons right away, but she feels they are on the right track.

Takeaway

Buying has evolved into a mindless effort that makes it challenging for anyone to distinguish wants versus needs. Taking steps to recognize the difference and change the approach and patterns to buying can lead to significant life improvements.

What's one small step you can take today?

19

The Power of Calendars & Reflection

The Challenge

I feel like I never know where everyone is supposed to be. I constantly fear being late or missing a meeting or appointment, because each family member has so much to do. Posting calendars to the refrigerator is no use to us. How can I get everyone in the family into an electronic calendar groove?

Harper's Story

The kids continue to get even busier with school. Between after-school activities, sports, sleepovers, and hanging out with friends, there are many dates and times to manage.

I also keep my days packed with my never-ending to-do list. For years, I kept a calendar and to-do list in a purse-sized notebook. Although I've moved to my email's calendar function to store everything, now there is digital clutter on my calendar, with so many kid activities and personal appointments combined.

With the kids having smartphones, maybe there is a better way to coordinate, so everyone knows what others are doing. I feel so stupid about this. My old notebook method worked great when I was in charge of all activities—but that isn't the case now.

Taking Action

Electronic calendars can revolutionize your life and help keep track of everything going on. A fundamental approach: Pick one calendar system and stick to it across all devices in the family.

Once you have selected an option (Outlook, Google, Apple, etc), consider creating individual calendars or color tags to toggle between activities. Calendars are easiest to set up from the computer first (rather than the phone) if using multiple overlapping calendars. For example:

Calendar	Content	Share
Personal	Doctor and personal appointments	Spouse (optional)
Spouse Personal	Doctor and personal appointments	Spouse (optional)
Individual children (one calendar each)	Doctor and school appointments and schedule	Parents and specific child
Financial	Bill reminders and savings goals	Spouse
Family & Friends	All social events for the entire family	Everyone in the family
Surprise	Gift-giving, planning surprises	No one?

With multiple calendars, you can manage who gets visibility over which calendars. With every calendar assigned a color, events can pop out on the calendar screen. These calendar events can hold shopping lists, appointment notes, and addresses to destinations (which is helpful when heading out with a mobile device).

In most systems, you can use the reminder or tasks feature to keep a running "to-do list" anchored with dates, which can also appear on a specific calendar. In addition, consider leveraging placeholder blocks to ensure there is time for things that could slip through the cracks (morning practices, taking walks, exercising, paying bills regularly, and more).

Sharing certain calendars is critical, so everyone in the family can see potential conflicts among appointments and events. Although these calendars can be available on the computer, phone, and watch, not all events need an alert. Think about the fatigue from those dopamine rushes every time an alarm goes off for everyone in the family.

Having the full suite of calendars available provides a view of how busy the family is as a whole. Is there downtime on any evening or weekend? Is everyone rushing from event to event? Stepping back both weekly and monthly to evaluate can bring better balance to everyone's lives.

Ways to Get Started

Making calendaring simple and easy for everyone to use is the fastest way to get the family on board. One or two missed activities or conflicts of events can help set the stage to get everyone to buy in on working together.

Camryn

Camryn's daughter committed to joining a friend on their family outing on a weekend Camryn and the girls were already going to be traveling. Camryn wants her daughters to do a better job of coordinating activities. She asks them what they use at school for calendaring, thinking it will be easier to extend that tool to their home life. Their school uses the Google platform, so Camryn decides to leverage her free Google account. Although she can quickly pick up how to use the calendar, it is sweet to have her girls give her a lesson in using the calendar and its features.

Next, Camryn looks at everything personal she has loaded on her work calendar to determine how many calendars she wants. She doesn't want to go crazy, but wants a multiple-calendar function to be of benefit. Camryn notes she would need a personal calendar for herself, one for each daughter, and one for "home" (which includes bill reminders, friends' birthdays, and other events). The girls demonstrate how Camryn can "share" the calendars between them. Now sharing is available on all but the home calendar.

Camryn scrolls back to the beginning of the month and begins loading anything personal on her work calendar into her

Google calendar. She sets up recurring appointments and loads both reminders and "to-do" items. She then removes these details from her work calendar and only notes "Personal Appt" when she has conflicts from events listed on the various family calendars.

Finally, Camryn and the girls confirm they can see the correct calendars on one another's phones. Loading these shared calendars means they do not have to invite each other to events, but they must log an event on their calendar so everyone in the family can see it. It is a relief to Camryn to no longer be the keeper of all family plans and information. Better yet, her older daughter immediately starts checking the calendars before even asking if she can do something with her friends.

Jade

Jade feels like they are running around with too much to do. Her husband set them up with a shared calendar on their phones, so she doesn't understand why everyone can't see how busy they are—and yet they continue to add activities.

One day in a store, Jade spots a large, spiral-bound monthly paper calendar. It is partly a calendar and partly a coloring book for adults. On impulse, she purchases it, but regrets it once she gets home, since she has no reason for this type of calendar. Jade realizes she misses the days of large desk calendars, where you could glance down and see everything (plus doodle on it).

At the end of the month, she begins flipping through this spiral calendar with its outlined pictures, and thinks about transferring her electronic calendar to paper for next month. It is not a super creative task, but she grabs a set of bright gel pens and jots the events down with different colors. This activity allows her mind to wander. Jade starts to connect the dots mentally around events, people, and tasks. Using the empty square at the bottom of the page, she creates a "to-do list" as tasks pop into her head.

With this month's view, Jade takes a fresh look at everything going on for her family. Are they overcommitted to events? Is there a lot of travel in the month? Do some days look tough to accomplish? Is "busyness" taking over, or is there a sense of balance? She wonders how she can tackle these concerns now, rather than waiting until she, or the family, is stressed out.

Jade also recognizes the act of this calendar transfer helped her look at empty blocks of time and consider her self-care. Does she have time in the month specifically set aside for her own care or a personal goal? Jade reviews the month again—is there any time on the calendar to be together as a family, or are events creating a hectic lifestyle? Jade feels empowered that she can discuss and correct their plans as a family using this bird's-eye view.

Harper

When the kids were little, Harper had a huge kitchen wall calendar to teach them days and months and learn about their upcoming activities. At that time, she kept it faithfully updated and enjoyed walking by and seeing what was going on with the family.

Now with everyone using their phones, she has no central calendar with visibility over everything. The school sends home various calendars for events, sports, and after-school activities, all of which Harper tries to note on her own calendar. Then she adds in their church activities and notes her husband's travel schedule.

But most of this is on her calendar. Several times there have been conflicts with her own activities, her husband's schedule, and what her two boys are doing in sports. This leaves someone rushing to pick up a child from practice or scramble to get from one event to another. This conflict is becoming more and more frustrating for everyone.

Harper decides getting in sync is a family task. One Sunday at dinner, she has everyone take turns going around the table and noting all evening and weekend plans. As a group, they immediately spot a few jammed days and discuss as a family if there is any flexibility in anyone's plans. This doesn't take long, but relieving the potential conflicts is a relief for everyone.

This becomes a standard family practice to quickly run through the upcoming week at every Sunday dinner. Harper is pleased with everyone's willingness to review what is coming up and pinpointing priorities.

 Nadia

Nadia and her wife are good at keeping each other informed regarding work-related and personal appointments. But now with the kids, there is an extra layer of activity they had not factored in. It is becoming more and more challenging to stay on top of everything the kids are enrolled in, carpool arrangements, and events the children are invited to.

They decide to start an electronic calendar for their children's activities. This way they both have visibility, and no one parent has to own keeping it updated. Nadia prints their full calendar weekly and posts it by the coffee pot. Every morning, Nadia and her wife review both the day's and week's events to look for any concerns.

This process gives them time to discuss everything their children are involved in, and decide when it is too much. Nadia does not want them to be involved in so many activities that they don't have downtime to simply play at home. Nadia's wife notes her Wednesday nights never present a conflict, so she suggests they make that a family dinner and game night.

Nadia is relieved to not be the only one managing all the kids' activities. She also likes this new feeling of collaboration when making scheduling decisions for their family.

Takeaway

There is a balance between feeling enslaved to calendars, and simply feeling comfortable and on top of everything life throws your way. As you start a new year, a new month, or even a new week, look at your family's calendar for the entire time period to ensure everyone is on the same page for every day.

What's one small step you can take today?

20

Gaming as Connectivity

The Challenge

My child is an introvert, and it has been challenging to find ways for him to connect with others. I want him to find friends, but his desired mode of connection is internet gaming. With more friends online instead of in person, I worry he is learning poor behaviors from children I do not know. Am I compromising his well-being and putting him at risk?

Jade's Story

My son seems to have only one or two school friends, and high school has been a tough road. He loves experimenting with his choices in clothing, haircuts, and accessories, and this has led to being made fun of and in some circumstances bullied. I think these situations made him reluctant to be on school video during the COVID quarantine. However, I've noticed he likes to talk to his friends by the same video while gaming online.

For as many negative things I have read regarding kids and online gaming, I struggle to limit his gaming because of one thing: connectivity. Sometimes we implement restrictions and limit his time playing (especially for battle games, which are not a personal favorite). Then the COVID quarantine made engaging with others even more challenging. There was not much else he was interested in doing besides gaming.

We end up restricting video games as punishment. I pull the power cord if he doesn't complete his chores or is disrespectful. Occasionally I consider removing the gaming system completely, but my husband disagrees and suggests I pay more attention to our son's interactions in his games and his online chats with friends to understand how this environment promotes connectivity. He does not even know some of his gaming friends IRL (in real life).

I worry about bullying or inappropriate behavior online, though I know it is no different from what he has experienced in school situations. If we teach him how to deal with bullying in school, do the same strategies apply here?

Am I limiting my son's relationships by limiting the games? How do I reconcile the control of gaming with this connection to his friends in a way he is comfortable? I don't want this to become a sore spot between my son, my husband, and me.

Taking Action

Online gaming provides a chance to connect with others of all ages. With some planning and boundaries, this can be a positive path parents can support.

Self-Awareness and Boundaries

Online, kids can learn what behaviors are acceptable and unacceptable, while hopefully feeling safe at home. In this virtual environment, they can step away from situations without embarrassment. For example, players who can get frustrated in games may lash out verbally or within the game itself in message forums. Helping your child develop a go-to phrase like "Hey, I'm out" or "I gotta go" allows them to remove themselves and not engage or escalate behavior out of line with the situation. It can also lead to great discussions and teachable moments regarding others' choices, primarily when the players get worked up and tensions escalate.

Setting boundaries on time and behavior, as well as teaching ways to handle these situations, are great life lessons. In addition, online game platforms have mechanisms to escalate truly improper behavior, which can even lead to removing that player from the forum.

For example, if your child experiences a player cheating, or using foul language or offensive names, they can report this through the in-game support chat or the platform's reporting tools. Teaching kids to correctly use these avenues can empower them to recognize inappropriate behaviors—like bullying—and how they should be addressed.

Long-Distance Friendships

Another benefit of online gaming is supporting long-distance friendships, as the virtual environment allows for global connection. Though they have different cultures and experiences, players engage through common activities.

In these games, they can work as teams to rescue the treasure; build lands, houses, and cities; and share experiences. They can connect online (whether directly in a game or via video call) while working virtually together. This connectivity allows them to develop their relationships.

Ways to Get Started

When your child finds a gaming platform (and community) they are interested in, it is an opportunity to set some boundaries, such as length of playing time. It is easy to lose all sense of time in these virtual worlds. After determining what time of day most friends are online or available, it is possible to restrict playing hours to that timeframe and limit the time to a mutually agreed upon length.

Some gaming forums have challenges that can encourage longer playing timeframes. This gives parents the chance to discuss which challenges are acceptable and the rules to participate (such as frequency of challenges, lengths of breaks, or time for sleep if it is an overnight challenge). Parents and children must also agree to what the consequences are for violating these rules.

With open dialogue and the ability to discuss difficult situations, online gaming can provide many lessons in human behavior and the strategies needed to manage personal reactions.

Camryn

Only one of Camryn's two daughters is interested in gaming. She loves the simulated city and community environments where she interacts with others. Camryn continues discussions with her daughter about how people behave in these environments. She also checks in with her daughter weekly on what she has experienced to discuss what is and isn't appropriate.

Camryn finds it difficult to not simply disregard what her daughter creates because it is in a video game. Her daughter develops interesting rooms, houses, and characters: no different from drawing or painting on paper. Camryn reminds herself to take the time to listen to her daughter as she shows off her creativity.

 Jade

Jade's husband enjoys gaming with his son in team games. When his son was younger, they played together in the family room, and he could monitor and discuss his son's behavior when the games got particularly challenging or frustrating.

Now his son is older and plays games with his friends on his computer in his room. Jade and her husband listen from their family room for their son getting particularly animated or frustrated. When it sounds like their son is losing patience, they have him end his game and come out of his room to get a change of scenery. Jade and her husband use that as a chance to reinforce when is a good time to step away or what to do when someone may be acting out of line.

Their son also struggles with time restrictions they have set, especially when friends can play for much longer or much later into the night. As parents, they try to be more flexible on the weekends or if out-of-state friends are available and their son wants to connect. However, if their son can't comply with the house rules like getting chores done before gaming, Jade's husband turns off internet access to the gaming system and computer.

Even with these challenges, Jade smiles when she hears her son genuinely laughing as he engages with others in his games. Despite Jade viewing the activity as a hobby, her son is now asking about a game programming elective he would like to take at school to learn how to build video games. Jade realizes there may be even more to gaming than fun and friendships.

Harper

Harper has strict rules about the length of time in front of any device. She shuts down and unplugs the computer itself, keeping the power cable hidden until she grants her child screen time again.

For her daughter, she allows limited tablet time, and then removes it for the day. Harper is trying to make screen time one of many activities available to her kids: not the only thing to do.

Harper's daughter protests that her friends have more devices and get to stay on them longer. In many cases, her friends have no restrictions on device time or applications. Her daughter feels she is missing out on chat messages and playing virtually with her friends.

This is frustrating for Harper, as it makes her daughter "different," but she knows these restrictions are the right thing for her family. She and her husband have discussed their approach several times to remain on the same page when reinforcing the rules.

Nadia

Nadia is coming to grips with the dependency her children will have on devices as they grow. Immediately in first grade, her daughter is taught to work with a tablet for educational content. Nadia purchases one for home, but currently, when her daughter is on the device, Nadia stays nearby to observe and talk to her daughter about what she is doing as well as monitor the amount of "tablet time" in a day.

Both Nadia and her wife fight the urge to hand it over simply to keep their daughter occupied, but it is always a struggle. For now, she tries to track how much time her daughter spends on the tablet, so she and her wife can continue to discuss what is appropriate.

Nadia resents the amount of work she invests in managing this device—and it is only one device for one child. But she believes if she sets (and evolves) these expectations and controls when her children are young, they won't be surprised by restrictions when they get older.

Takeaway

When your child is interested in online gaming, game development, or robotics, this doesn't have to mean they are isolated. They can still create a community with others, make critical friend connections, and learn acceptable social boundaries with your guidance and monitoring.

Gaming exposes children to a larger group of people than they would meet or interact with locally. This means there are many opportunities to discuss poor sportsmanship, being a friend, and how human nature deals with winning and losing.

What's one small step you can take today?

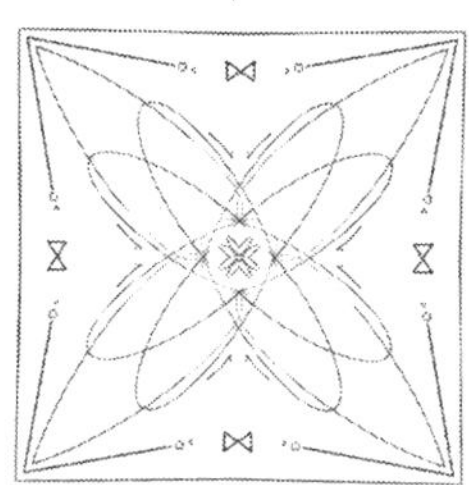

21

SELF-CARE: Spa Alternatives

The Challenge

As my friends describe their spa days, I want to relax and enjoy that kind of self-care activity, but I'm so nervous. I want to find something I am comfortable with, and a spa experience is not what I imagine for myself.

Harper's Story

The moms I interact with talk about their wonderful spa visits for things like massages, skin scrubs, and body wraps. I never considered that kind of self-care. I'm uncomfortable with the idea of a fancy spa treatment. It seems somewhat indulgent and expensive. But now, with juggling kids, my parents' care, and life in general, maybe having the ability to relax like that should be a priority?

A spa sounds like too much work with the precautions necessary today. If I'm worried about health and safety, I won't find it a relaxing experience. My friend, who understands my reluctance, gave me a "pod" gift certificate for my birthday. I can choose between a heated salt-water pod or warm-air pod to relax in. I'm not sure what I am getting into, but I trust my friend and it doesn't involve anyone else, so maybe it's worth a try?

Taking Action

A private form of self-care can be individual pod therapies. Either water-based or air-based, these pods are usually housed in individual treatment rooms (sometimes with a private shower) and minimal interaction with staff.

Floating Away

If you are unfamiliar with this centuries-old form of relaxation, a float spa is the chance to soak in a tub of water heavily mixed with Epsom salts. This experience is called "floating" and is done in a "pod" in a private suite. Your pod allows you to close out all the distractions in the world and enjoy some light and musical ambiance. In the end, you rinse (and can wash your hair) in your float suite's private shower. If you find the ocean relaxing, this might be a good fit.

The Experience

What you will find floating:

- By lying weightless in water, your joints and muscles can relax.
- Absolutely any little scratch on your skin will be called to your attention in the salty water.
- If you are slightly claustrophobic and need a bit of cool air circulating, use a towel rolled up like a log to keep the pod cover open a bit.
- It's a personal choice to determine how much or how little you want to wear in your float (bathing suit or not).

This experience is more relaxing than a rigorous treatment, such as a deep tissue massage.

Warm and Snuggly

If water does not sound appealing, check out sauna therapy in a sauna pod. Unlike a common sauna room, this modern but private take on them can make the experience more comfortable. In a sauna pod, you can lie down in a heated chamber, which warms up and soothes muscles while your head is outside the pod, with cooler air blowing across your face.

In some pods, you can hook up a device to stream video content. Alternatively, you can relax and let your mind wander. Additional options in the pod are available, like gentle massage, where the unit lightly vibrates.

As you work up a sweat, you can close your eyes and feel transported to a tropical climate.

Ways to Get Started

With many alternatives to a traditional spa experience, there are many comfortable, affordable options.

 Harper

Harper is not much of a beach person, so she decides to try the sauna pod using her gift card. Worried the experience would be clinical or uncomfortable, she appreciates the elegant privacy once she is escorted to her pod room.

Although the room feels cool, as soon as she climbs into the pre-heated pod, the warmth surrounds her. Harper closes her eyes and listens to the piped-in nature sounds. Soon she finds herself drifting, not asleep but not quite awake.

When Harper finishes, she emerges and finds a clean, fluffy towel to dry off with. She also performs some basic stretches, enjoying how loose her muscles are. Harper is not known for napping, but the mental quietness leaves her feeling refreshed. She appreciates this new therapy and thinks it is something she would like to experience again.

Takeaway

As therapies continue to evolve, there are opportunities to meet everyone at their comfort level. It's important to find something that provides true personal benefits, not simply a collective trend.

What's one small step you can take today?

22

Attic Treasures as Gifts from the Heart

The Challenge

How can I enjoy sharing my family's stories and items with my kids, so the memories come to life and don't feel like a burden? These treasures piled in boxes and tubs are simply ignored and take up space.

Nadia's Story

I have a closet that reminds me of my childhood attic above the garage. At around eleven years old, I thought it was cool when my parents grabbed that just-in-reach cord and pulled down a folding ladder out of the ceiling.

I remember going up with my mom one early summer morning (before it got too hot). Crouched almost in half, I looked around at the mishmash of boxes, old appliances, tools, and other assorted bits spread across planks over the rafters. Mom immediately zeroed in on a stack of boxes labeled with her handwriting. I don't know what she was initially looking for, but before I could even comprehend the entire storage situation, Mom had pulled the lids off, sat down, and started revisiting old memories.

These boxes contained all kinds of items I had never seen before, including:

- *A cloth napkin from the fancy restaurant mom and dad went to for prom.*
- *Paper doll cutouts wrapped in faded newspaper.*
- *Piles of old coins from European countries.*
- *Large plastic horses of various breeds that used to be on the shelves of her childhood bedroom.*

Even as I listened to my mom's stories, two thoughts kept swirling:

- *Why have I never seen this stuff before?*
- *Why do we have to sit in a dusty, stale attic to enjoy these things?*

Now, those same items sit in boxes stacked high in my closet. I mean, this is valuable storage space in our small home, but what can I do with it all? Throwing it out seems like a violation, like I'm betraying the memories of my parents. But I'm not exactly filled with love when I open this closet door.

Taking Action

Evaluating what family mementos you have and how you can best enjoy them is critical to relieving the burden of accumulating and storing the family archives. It's a challenge to keep everything we treasure, but why not take pictures of those items and make a book, post the photo, tell a story, and share those memories without climbing a ladder or dusting off a box?

First, pull out and sort everything by person or timeframe. Is there any value (monetary or sentimental) in keeping the item, or would a photo of the item be enough? Photographing mementos (instead of saving them) can help free up space.

Ways to Get Started

Know what you have, first and foremost. Then you can start evaluating what to keep, document, and let go of.

Camryn

At the bottom of a box, Camryn finds some old black and white photographs of her family's hometown taken in the 1930s. These photos are charming, highlighting the architecture of buildings that still exist today. She decides to take her girls out on a sunny day and take pictures of these same urban scenes today.

Using the original photos as reference, Camryn finds it interesting to take the same picture in the same location where the surrounding buildings, roads, and spaces have evolved. Once these are captured, Camryn has the black and white photos scanned and assembles everything into a folder on her computer with the old and new photos side by side.

Camryn uses an online photo book company to make a small album, where each page simply shows the two images together. Knowing that these images are something her father would be interested in, she makes this book a Father's Day present.

As a lifelong resident of their town and former business owner in the construction industry, he is intimately familiar with most of these buildings. This simple gift is an instant hit, and for months he carries that album with him, sharing it with other retired construction colleagues.

Camryn is surprised this little photo book neither cost a lot nor was complicated to create. However, the sentimental value to her father is priceless.

Jade

When rearranging the basement (again) to make more storage space, Jade unearths the same box she has been lugging around for years. It is a set of ceramic dogs her mother collected during her childhood. Jade doesn't have the heart to get rid of the dogs, but she feels a pang of frustration every time she looks at this box.

Jade opens the box and again unwraps the dogs from faded tissue paper. She aligns them on top of another box to see them all together. Suddenly Jade discerns there are as many dogs as grandchildren on her mother's side of the family, and is inspired.

She reaches out to her siblings and asks if they would be comfortable breaking up the set, so each grandchild has something to remember their grandmother. Jade's siblings love the idea, especially since they do not remember the dog set. Jade snaps some pictures to text over, and everyone quickly agrees to the idea.

Jade selects new, bright red tissue paper and fancy green and gold ribbon to wrap each dog individually for the holidays. Wrapped identically, there can be no preference for which dog goes to which grandchild. It brings a warm rush to Jade's heart to know a box in the basement no longer annoys her. Now these items are bringing joy to more members of the family.

 Harper

Harper's husband reminds her that a box in their storage shed looks like it will fall apart. Harper knows it is a collection of vacation trinkets her family collected during her childhood. Each item brought her happy memories of summer vacation, but across the family, no one wants the box now.

Harper figures it's best to bring in the box, go through the trinkets, and send pictures to her siblings to see if they want an item. If not, the box should probably just go.

As she pulls the different items out, Harper's daughter comes over and starts investigating each one. Harper quickly rattles off where something came from, and roughly how old she was on each vacation. With each trinket, Harper smiles and recounts a quick story about her family that her daughter finds funny. Together, they enjoy items that had sat unnoticed for years.

Harper's daughter is intrigued by these items and all they represent about her relatives. She asks her mom if it is okay to display these on the bookcases in their family room. Harper doesn't see any harm in it, so she dusts them off, and her daughter positions them on the shelves. As Harper reviews the collection, she recognizes she has purchased similar pieces on their more recent vacations. She and her daughter scout around the house, pulling out vacation souvenirs of their own. They then mix in these newer memories with the older ones for display.

Harper is fascinated by how full circle she has come from her childhood vacations to those she plans for her family. The combined collection inspires joy and stories every time she looks at her bookcases. Harper tosses the wilting but empty box into the trash.

Nadia

Nadia decides she is taking charge of the various boxes of her childhood memorabilia in their guest bedroom closet, rather than possibly moving it all to a new home. She grabs an empty storage tub and decides she'll take a picture of whatever does not fit in that tub, then move on.

Once her tub is full, Nadia sets up a small corner in her family room where natural light shines in. She hangs a plain sheet over two chairs and sets the individual items on this clean backdrop one by one. Nadia quickly develops a rhythm of arranging an object and taking several pictures with her phone. When she is done, everything goes into a box to discard.

Nadia loads the photos onto her computer and renames the files, knowing which images correspond to which items. She then loads them into a photo gifts website and creates a collage to print and frame.

Nadia is so happy with the result that she has additional collages printed for her siblings as gifts. Now Nadia can enjoy seeing family treasures without them taking up space.

Takeaway

Storage space seems to be at a premium these days: The need for space takes over basements and garages, and people even sometimes need to rent additional storage space. Developing ways to remember family treasures without the guilt of the space they consume can make those items more present in your daily life.

What's one small step you can take today?

23

Alternative Holiday Traditions

The Challenge

Some of the large holiday traditions no longer align with my family. Often, I feel these are a lot of work for not much enjoyment. The kids are not invested in these traditions and would probably skip some if they could. I want to bring meaning and family ownership to these holidays.

Camryn's Story

For me, some holiday traditions no longer fit the way we live. On Thanksgiving, it is just the girls and me, so it feels silly to try to prepare an elaborate meal for three. But then I feel guilty I'm ignoring such a long-standing tradition.

Christmas doesn't seem to fit either. We don't have room for elaborate decorations, and the girls are bored with the same items we drag out year after year. It's not like they are little and waiting for the magic of Santa Claus.

Am I giving up as a mother by not working to make these traditions as grand as I should? Will they compare our holidays to their friends' families, who may do more elaborate events, and think I'm failing?

Taking Action

Traditions are at the core of holiday celebrations, but repeating practices without bringing in children to help own them leaves a gap in meaning and caring.

However, it can be difficult to institute new traditions when people cling to familiar ones. This change can be frightening to some family members, while others relish something new. There is a delicate balance to strike when looking to move traditions in a new direction.

In the United States, with many large holidays, there are many traditions to reexamine, modify, or even expand on, so all generations can enjoy.

Ways to Get Started

Due to the pandemic, the world has to look at holiday celebrations in new ways. Getting creative with holiday events can create new memories, and even abolish traditions that might be more toxic than treasured. Challenging families to think outside the box has the possibility of resetting holidays to be what they were meant to be: joyous.

In talking to friends or co-workers, there is an opportunity to learn about other cultures and traditions. Internet research can also help spark ideas. There is no right or wrong in creating, modifying, or extending a tradition. There is also no failure in trying something new that still might not seem to fit. The evolution of these holidays can make for great memories themselves.

Camryn

Camryn wants to bring a different energy to this upcoming Thanksgiving meal, particularly after days of gray and cold weather. She announces to the girls it will be a "tropical Thanksgiving" this year. Although met with surprised faces, she encourages the girls to think about how they can transform their small meal into something different.

Inspired by this direction, her youngest finds leftover tissue paper to form large tropical flowers as table decorations. Searching "palm frond templates" online, her daughter also cuts out leaves from green construction paper. The flowers and leaves combined make a lively runner of color down the center of the table, interspersed with white votive candles floating in small bowls of water.

Camryn is excited to introduce a turkey recipe with a buttered rum pineapple glaze. Using a small five-pound turkey, Camyrn thinks the juices involved in the recipe create the moistest turkey she's ever served. In addition, she cooks a citrus-infused stuffing, and her girls make a small piña colada cake.

Camryn's older daughter researches online and selects meal blessings from different cultures. She puts a different blessing at each place setting, and they each read theirs aloud to kick off dinner in a unique way. They all agree this has been a memorable Thanksgiving, and would like to continue to brainstorm and try it again next year.

 Jade

As part of their holiday decorations, Jade always sets out a picture frame with her kids on Santa's lap. That tradition has ended as they have grown older. Jade opens the rear of the frame and looks through all the stacked pictures of Santa visits through time. It is fun to see how the kids have changed year over year, yet Santa looks the same!

Jade thinks about her own Santa tradition as a child. Her family would get all dressed up and head to the largest department store downtown. The store would be transformed into a wonderland, which enchanted her and her siblings. Jade digs around for her own Santa pictures to recall those visits.

As she digs, Jade finds beautiful black and white pictures of her mother, aunts, and uncles visiting Santa many decades ago. It is fascinating to see this tradition go back three generations. Jade decides to take advantage of having all these photos readily available.

She has the photos scanned and builds a small photo album online with a cute holiday template. She only places one image on each page, noting the year. Jade prints the book, and wraps it when it arrives.

On Christmas Eve, this solitary gift appears under the tree after dinner. Her son quickly opens it and sits with his sister, flipping through each page. They are shocked at the young pictures of their grandmother, and laugh at the images of their mom and her siblings. They can't believe their expressions in some of their own Santa pictures, and begin telling stories of their visits.

As the extended family gathers on Christmas day, the "Santa Book," as it is now called, is the most popular item to share. Every family member flips through it and shares even more stories. Jade thinks about how simple it is to pull together these photos across generations, and is happy at the joy it brings to others. She knows she will bring this photo book out only at Christmas to share again.

Harper

Harper always sets up the Christmas tree with their traditional ornaments, bows, and a combination of green and red lights. The kids have lost interest in decorating. Harper is pleased with how the tree looks when she is done, but the kids do not pay any attention. She is sad the kids do not seem to care about the tree.

Her son mentions it is "Mom's tree" because Mom determines the colors, ornaments, and theme. The kids wholly disassociate with this tradition. Harper thinks back to her childhood, where they had a professionally decorated tree. She remembers how disappointing she found it. Now, she realizes she is repeating this same disappointment with her children.

This year, after they bring the tree into the family room, she asks the kids where it should go. Everyone looks at her, surprised. This wasn't usually a consideration. When she permits the kids to think a bit differently, they entertain a host of ideas. Finally, they all agree they are willing to move a bit of furniture to put the tree in a new spot in front of a picture window. It is the opposite side of the room from where the tree normally is, but after scooting the furniture around a bit, it becomes picturesque.

Next, Harper asks what colors to use on the tree. She lets each child pick a color, but requests the colors not be too outrageous. Harper is delighted when the kids discuss and announce they would like to do a silver, blue, and white-themed tree with white lights.

Harper agrees, and the kids become energized. She takes them to the local home and garden center, where she gives the kids three things to look for in the colors they had planned: regular round bulbs of various sizes, ribbon or garland, and one unique ornament they each individually select. The kids take off with the shopping cart, and Harper shops for the white lights. They meet at the checkout line, and the cart has everything Harper asked for.

At home, decorating the tree becomes a full family affair, complete with holiday music playing. It is clear the kids are enjoying the effort, which transforms the start of the Christmas holiday for everyone. Stepping back, the tree looks beautiful and seems to have radically changed their family room. The kids begin talking about their color options for the following year, and Harper smiles at the new tradition.

Nadia

Nadia is happy to host the large Thanksgiving meal this year, but she knows the hosting usually takes away from the visiting. Other years, she enjoys hearing stories from her remaining grandparents, along with her parents and siblings. Since Nadia will be busy in the kitchen before dinner, she creates a more lasting opportunity to capture these stories.

Nadia puts out a name tag at every seat at the adult table. Next to each tag is a small card with a year written at the top. As the family arrives, she encourages each person to jot down a family story from the year indicated on the card. The story doesn't have to be long or elaborate, but something that would be fun to share.

Nadia does not believe how seriously her family takes this assignment. She hears some quiet chatter, but family members are mostly bent over their laps, writing down something they remember. Nadia also appreciates her oldest niece sitting with her great-grandmother and taking down what she says.

As they finish, everyone drops their cards into a basket. Following dinner, the oldest nieces and nephews are tasked with clearing the table. As they do, Harper walks around the table with the basket, and every adult selects a card. Kids return to the dining room, and the adults review their cards. They read a story aloud; then the original author chimes in with additional details. The laughter ensues, while memories long forgotten come out.

Harper enjoys the new stories that emerge, taking the place of the same ones they usually repeat year after year. She is also delighted to have these stories captured, and knows she will do something special with them at some point. Adults quickly ask if this can be a tradition to repeat in future years.

Takeaway

The power of tradition can be a tough thread to unravel, but traditions must evolve as families do before they become outdated, unfit, and possibly miserable memories. New traditions may ultimately bring more meaning to holidays.

What's one small step you can take today?

24

Alternative Birthday Traditions

The Challenge

Birthday parties seem to evolve over time, from children inviting their entire class to teenagers barely participating with their families. How can I make birthdays special for the individual person in a way that feels comfortable for them?

 Nadia's Story

I love making birthdays special, but it's challenging, as the expectation seems to change over time. As little kids, it's all about parties and activities with classmates year-round. But with my older nieces and nephews, it boils down to sending gift cards; the "celebrations" cease.

I never want any birthday to be about gifts. I want birthdays to be a true celebration of each family member's presence in the world and their lives—no matter their age.

I look around at my little family, and I wonder if we could create some kind of birthday tradition that will last through the years. I don't know what they will want to do as they get older, but it is important to me to help them understand how much I value their being here.

Taking Action

With changes in how we gather and celebrate, alternative ideas may become lifelong traditions. It's a matter of getting creative.

Sibling Dates

One approach to some dedicated time is a "sibling birthday dinner," where siblings can spend an evening having a great dinner—with no spouses and no children. The birthday person can select the restaurant; the other siblings split the bill. It is incredible how the focused time allows for lively conversation, reflection, and laughter! No presents need to be involved, but exchanging (usually hilarious) cards can be enough.

These dates let you try new restaurants in your city or attend a festival. The birthday person selecting the venue or activity can reflect their personality, but they can share with the others.

Birthday Dates

Another take on this can be a "birthday date" for children. An individual parent (mother and son or father and daughter) can select a time to engage one-on-one, like a traditional date. For young children, this may start with a dinner at McDonald's. Later, they may graduate to dinner and a movie. Through the years, there can be a progression to nicer and nicer restaurants, more mature films, and sometimes alternative activities like gallery tours, lectures, dancing, sporting events, shows, and more. This tradition can continue to adapt into adulthood.

Within families, siblings may have different definitions of date activities. As children get older, this can even include traveling. Consider this time as a special chance to catch up one-on-one and reflect on your lives as a parent and child (and the move to grandparent and parent!).

Giving to Yourself and Others

In other circumstances—the family may not be physically close—birthdays present the opportunity for self-reflection. Whether going on a retreat or a walk in nature, the day can be considered a day of sacred celebration for yourself.

Another option is to give yourself as a gift to others. Volunteering can bring you an emotional reward while giving to others on your special day.

Ways to Get Started

There are various ways to connect using your birthday as a catalyst. Creating a tradition around this can bring more meaning to your day of birth and your meaningful relationships.

Camryn

Camryn's days are so busy, and evenings are jammed with activities. As much as her daughters, family, and friends want to make her birthday a big deal or event, Camryn would like to use her birthday to pause. This day can give her time to look back and look forward while being with her family.

As her birthday approaches and her girls want to make plans, Camryn tells them how she would prefer to create a mini-retreat. She wants to get out of the city and take the girls on a hike, followed by an early dinner. Camryn saw the confusion in the girls' faces by not wanting a "party," but in her heart, Camryn knows this respite is what she truly wants as a gift.

Camryn hunts online and finds a nearby state park with some easy trails. They wake up early one Saturday, grab coffee and hot chocolates, and head out. They spend most of the morning and early afternoon hiking and looking at the world around them. Sometimes they are chatting, but often they are quiet, simply taking it all in.

Afterwards, they find a tiny mom-and-pop restaurant in a small town and enjoy a relaxing early dinner. One daughter even sneaks away (with the pretense of going to the restroom) to tell the owners about Camryn's birthday. Camryn is surprised when a piece of pie arrives at the table with a candle in it. Camryn feels this day is a real celebration, as well as a beautiful chance for connection: It's a tradition she'd like to repeat annually.

Jade

Jade doesn't want anything for her birthday. Her family keeps asking her for ideas, but nothing comes to mind. Jade is pretty good about going shopping when she wants something, but she has a new passion for reducing her purchases, so asking for things doesn't appeal to her.

When Jade receives an online charity donation request from a friend, she starts to think about what charities have meaning for her. Is there a charity where she feels her contribution could make a difference? Jade lists five charities that touch her, and puts the names in a bowl. At dinner, she announces to her family she would like to donate to three charities for her birthday instead of receiving anything. Her husband holds the bowl, while Jade and her children each draw a name. Everyone seems energized by this idea of giving.

On the morning of her birthday, Jade finds a card sitting next to her teacup in the kitchen. Inside, not only did her family write birthday wishes, but they also noted the donations they made in Jade's name to all five charities she originally listed. Jade is touched that her family generously gave to charities she found important. She knows this is a birthday tradition she'll continue.

Harper

Harper is reaching a milestone birthday, and she knows there are plans for a celebration. She thinks back to all the birthday parties her family has created. They are large, chaotic, and fun, but there is only time for chit-chat with family members: no real conversation.

Harper reaches out to her two siblings and requests a birthday dinner for just the three of them. At first, there is slight pushback about finding time for another event in addition to her party, but Harper insists.

She picks a restaurant where they can enjoy a nice meal on a pretty patio. It seems awkward at first; her siblings expect Harper to share some big news. But all Harper wants is a chance to connect. Everyone starts talking about their children, work, and parents. It is a great conversation. As they relax, they talk about their latest favorite movies, vacations, and by dessert, they are discussing random pop culture. Instinctively, no one wants to talk about news, politics, or anything that brings conflict or consternation to the evening.

At the end of the night, Harper's sister jokes her birthday is next, and she expects the same sibling attention. As they laugh, they agree. Why not? A chance to connect is rare in their busy lives. Making a "sibling date" for the next birthday makes sense.

Harper comes home elated, charged up from time spent with the people she has known the longest. Her kids keep asking her about the significance of this new tradition, and Harper explains how difficult it is to connect when everyone has families and activities of their own. Later, Harper hears her children discussing where they would go if they held sibling birthday dates.

Nadia

Now that they are reaching the end of the baby cake-smashing birthdays, Nadia wonders if there is some kind of birthday tradition her family can create and look forward to for themselves. Her kids move on to friend parties, but these seem like more work than enjoyment for the parents. The kids are too young for fancy dinners out, and they wouldn't eat anything on the menu anyway.

Nadia decides to try a birthday brunch on her own birthday. Brunch gives the family a chance to dress up and go someplace lovely, but still eat pancakes (while the birthday mom enjoys a mimosa).

Nadia and her spouse enjoy the birthday brunch as much as the kids. They quickly realize this seems like a great birthday tradition for all their birthdays—and something that can grow with their children.

Takeaway

Some people relish birthdays; others would prefer to downplay the event. However, everyone deserves to feel acknowledged and appreciated. Consider a gift to yourself by introducing a new tradition on your birthday!

What's one small step you can take today?

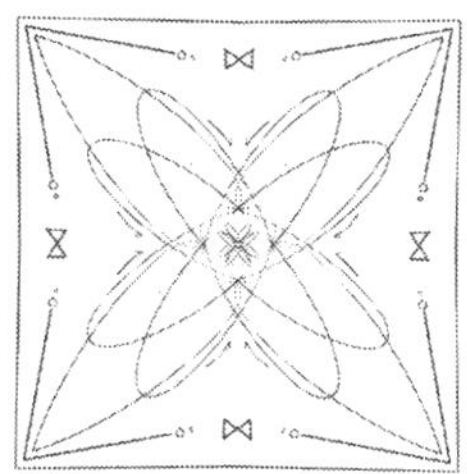

25

Friend Networking

The Challenge

Each week, I think I'll have the time to catch up with friends, extended family, even coworkers, but the time never seems to materialize. Now, I'm hesitant to even try due to periods of isolation and distance.

Harper's Story

My time is at a premium, with an endless list of activities and tasks rolling over from day to day. The days always start to merge, and pretty soon, it seems like weeks have gone by, and I have not connected with anyone outside my family unless they are part of my to-do list. But the kids are starting to do more with their friends, and I realize my time is opening up a bit.

I have made my family my top priority over the past few years, so my social circle is pretty small. I volunteer with people, but I do not think of them as girlfriends to call and hang out with. I struggle to make that connection. I believe in the value of networks, but I'm feeling kind of alone in my daily life and lacking emotional support outside my marriage. Facebook isn't my idea of connecting with people. I need more from a real-life social network, but I don't know where to start. Do I have to rebuild my friend network from scratch?

Taking Action

Friend networking can and should be a high priority: no different than professional networking. Friendships can ebb and flow over time, throughout various points in everyone's lives. However, it is easy to get caught up in daily living and suddenly realize it has been too long since you've connected with others. In addition, with prolonged isolation, researchers now find that people are experiencing "stress-induced social avoidance."

Professional networking is considered extremely important. However, personal one-on-one chats, where the focus is on catching up, are a wonderfully comfortable and powerful activity with friends. With acquaintances, taking the time to learn more about someone else is a new personal investment. Creating "conversation dates" can help you to expand your trusted social circle.

Even knowing how wonderful a good conversation with another interested person can feel, it can still be intimidating to pick up the phone or send an email or text to someone to create a conversation date—especially if it's been too long. Things may have changed so much for you or your friend, so it can be scary to reach out.

Setting up a little challenge can be motivating and bring about change. What if you committed to one conversation date a week? It could be breakfast, lunch, virtual coffee, or happy hour. It could be a friend you have not connected with for a while, or an acquaintance you want to know better, who may even become a friend. It may take some effort to schedule this time, but after a while, it can become a routine you look forward to and don't want to miss.

The Meeting

No expectations should be set for these meetings, as there is no ulterior motive. To stay curious, lead with questions such as: "What have you been doing?" "How have you been feeling?" By going into a conversation with no other goal, you may be surprised when something magical can happens. Whether someone connects you with a friend or colleague, a friend offers sage advice, or you just experience a load of laughter, you may leave feeling more fulfilled than when you arrived (and they may as well!).

In some cases, an older friendship may not return to its original state. That's okay. Show up as a friend and determine the natural progress of the relationship.

Ways to Get Started

Develop a running list of five to ten people to connect with, so you can be guaranteed to set something up each week. Add to your list as people pop up in your mind, or as you meet new people at different events for work or just in your daily life.

Take time on Sundays to look over your calendar for the next two weeks and think about who you would like to connect with.

Another thing to consider is what days and times work well for you to meet. What are your options? This can help you work a conversation date into your routine each week. Are Wednesday evenings and Saturday mornings your most ideal time to meet? Create some predictability and consistency around your time, so you can meet your goal of a connection per week.

You can track the progress of reaching out by noting who you heard back from and if any time is set up to connect. You might not hear back from someone one month but they become more available the next month. Being patient and respectful will pay off.

Camryn

Camryn knows she has an extensive professional network. With various career experiences, she has trusted relationships she continues to cultivate. Yet looking around, she feels her friend group is pretty sparse. It seems like friends come and go in her life. So often, there is a happy or intense relationship for a time, but it eventually dissipates. Camryn is disappointed in herself for letting these relationships wane.

Camryn decides to focus on local relationships that could use a jump start. Looking over her schedule, she realizes she has the most flexibility on Sundays. She blocks off time at 10:00 a.m. and 2:00 p.m. and begins reaching out. Camryn states what is in her heart: She is sorry their existing relationship lapsed, and would they be interested in connecting over coffee?

Camryn never knows what to expect with these meetings, which is a scary but wonderful feeling. She wants to listen and learn, find out what is happening in a friend's life, and develop a way to keep the connection more robust.

In some instances, she has friends who said they are interested in getting together, but continue to postpone or reschedule. Knowing how times in people's lives vary, Camryn notes in her contacts when it's not a good time for a specific person, and makes a note to try again later. Camryn has to work to remind herself there is nothing personal in these delays. The immediate issues in someone's life take precedence over anything else. In the meantime, the relationships she continues to develop with friends who she can connect with fill her up with joy.

Jade

Jade has a small circle of friends, primarily from college. They are her most significant friendships, but they are scattered all over the country. Jade likes their updates on social media to express her continued thoughts for them, but over time, it doesn't seem enough. Since they are all the same age, Jade is curious whether they are facing the same challenges. How nice would it be to talk to someone who can relate firsthand?

Jade begins reaching out via instant message to coordinate virtual happy hours. She starts with one or two of her closest friends to see if it even works. There is no strategy or goal outside of bringing your favorite beverage to a virtual meet-up. She sets the expectation of an hour or less, but after a few sessions, she realizes they're chatting for much longer!

Over time, Jade and her friends decide to broaden their happy hours and begin meeting virtually twice a month. The group takes turns inviting one person to join them. Whether it's an additional friend or someone new, it doesn't matter. Jade begins to look forward to these chats and makes scheduling around them a priority. Everyone agrees it is come-as-you-are. Whether dressed for work or in their pajamas, the connection is the priority. Jade regrets not thinking of this earlier. She relishes the positive influence it has on her life.

Harper

With Harper's busy volunteering schedule, she feels connected with everyone in her small town on an acquaintance level. She can't go to the store without stopping to say hello to several people. Yet when she needs a friend to talk to, Harper doesn't feel close to anyone outside her family.

Since Harper works best with an ongoing to-do list, she adds "Mom Meet-Ups" to the list. Harper selects different spots around town: coffee shop, park, or even a playground if she knows someone has young kids to watch. She tries to connect her volunteer activities with these meet-ups: inviting someone from her church group and someone from the school parent-teacher organization.

By focusing on connecting with two other people instead of one, Harper gets to learn more about the people she interacts with, but removes the nervousness she would feel meeting one-on-one.

Sometimes these triads have a lot in common, other times very little. But the exposure deepens their connections. More often than not, Harper or another person feel a strong connection and feel more comfortable to reach out further for one-on-one time. Over time, Harper believes her small town is swelling with relationships she never thought possible.

Nadia

Nadia is drowning in mommy time. With small kids, everything revolves around their schedule. It is more challenging than she ever expected—so many other things she used to care about now fall to the side. Her need for adult conversations is real! As her daughter begins a regular school schedule, Nadia tries to think of ways to bring some of that connection back to her life.

Nadia remembers reading about professionals and their "walking meetings." Instead of sitting in a room, these business-people hold small meetings while walking around their business campus or nearby green space. Nadia feels that could be the best of both worlds: being a little more active and connecting with someone else.

Nadia reaches out to a fellow mom with whom she interacts regularly. They see each other at the same school events, organizations, and activities. Nadia texts the idea of a stroller walk and talk. As soon as she presses send, she becomes embarrassed. Would it make sense to anyone else? Do others feel it is a waste of time? No sooner did she have these thoughts than her phone buzzed, with the mom enthusiastically accepting the idea! It's a relief someone else feels that same need to connect.

After the first walk and talk, Nadia is invigorated. She looks over the family calendar and believes she can schedule this twice a week in the mornings, after school drop-off, but before other appointments and activities kick into gear. Nadia invites other mothers based on their availability. The fresh air, the exercise, and the connection boost Nadia's mental and physical state.

Takeaway

Relationships take work, no different than anything else in life. Without attention, they can fall away and be difficult to resurrect. Creating a strategy of mindful, deliberate opportunities to connect can develop relationships and even negate the distance created by busy lives.

What's one small step you can take today?

26

Growing with Coaching

The Challenge

As my kids transition to other stages of their lives, I feel my life is transitioning too. However, I feel lost in determining what exactly that change should be, and how I would make it. I don't even know who to talk to that could help me make these kinds of changes.

Sometimes I drift through my own life. My kids are growing and changing, and yet I feel stagnant. Ideas and goals I had years ago don't seem to fit now. I'm unsure what is next for me.

I try to talk to friends and siblings about this lack of focus, but most do not have much to contribute except that I should "hang in there" and I will "figure things out."

Finally, a friend suggested I find a life coach. After "googling" and reading what a life coach was, the more interested I became. Would working with a coach help me identify next steps in my life? I fear life is racing by and not feeling satisfied.

Taking Action

Partnering with a coach in any area of your life can bring about tactical change. Unlike a therapist, who works through the history of your life to determine your actions and feelings, a coach can bring focus, energy, and strategies to move you along a path. A coach can help identify strengths, interests, and opportunities to inspire and accomplish change.

Coaches usually have specific expertise, and different coaches can work with you at various stages of your life. Common areas coaches can help with include:

- Career change
- Relationship development (personal or professional)
- Health, wellness, and fitness
- Leadership development
- Breaking habits (drinking, smoking)

By identifying the area you would like to work on, finding the right coach is similar to finding the right doctor or therapist. You have to find someone you are comfortable with and trust.

Ways to Get Started

Finding the right coach can take some time. Referrals can be the best way to start: someone you trust connecting you with someone they are happy working with. Coaches should be as interested in finding the right fit as you are. It is essential to interview a coach to ensure a strong connection and level of trust. Without a relationship and rapport, no great ideas will be successfully implemented.

Even with a strong relationship, a coaching agreement should be specific about steps to take and the length of time expected. At the outset, a shorter agreement should be the starting point to confirm the relationship and outcomes are aligned.

Camryn

Camryn feels her career needs a boost. She has quickly moved up the ladder at her company, but she is no longer sure she wants to climb much higher. She has learned that moving up to the C-suite is less about doing a good job and delivering results, and more about playing politics, which she despises.

Camryn knows she has extensive professional skills and experience in various business situations, but she is not sure what that adds up to and what direction it can take her. When Camryn mentions this to a friend in Human Resources, the friend recommends a career coach she knows.

Camryn feels uncomfortable reaching out to a coach without a plan or understanding of what she would do next. However, when meeting, the coach does not seem surprised or worried about the lack of a specific focus to start. She explains this is part of the journey—determining what Camryn enjoys, what she does best, and what that means professionally. Camryn immediately feels relieved she doesn't have to provide the answers going in.

Through a series of assessments and conversations, Camryn zeros in on what she truly values in a career and what that represents in the workplace. Through the work with her coach, Camryn can see that as her experience has expanded, her current job no longer fits her desires. As a specific career path develops, Camryn reaches out to her professional network to see how she can move in that direction. It does not take long for Camryn to shift into a career that brings her the fulfillment she is looking for.

 Jade

Some days Jade feels she is destined for great things. There has to be something she can offer the world, her community, and her family, but she can't put her finger on it. She has a nagging sensation she tries to ignore, but it doesn't go away.

In a short window of time, the idea of working with a life coach keeps surfacing. She sees a piece on television about it, then she reads something about a life coach in an online news story. Even in her social media feed, life coaching came up. Jade feels something is pointing her in that direction.

First, Jade begins in a life coaching group—women looking for the next chapter in their lives. After months of interaction, the opportunity to work directly with the group's coach develops. Again, Jade feels it is something she is supposed to do, so she begins an individual coaching engagement.

At first, it is jarring. The coach can zero in on weaknesses (Jade saw them as flaws) that can be developed into strengths. These weaknesses currently limit Jade's ability to navigate change. However, with a series of activities and exercises, Jade feels she is developing mental and emotional muscles she's never had before.

This boost in confidence and self-identification leads Jade to explore areas she never thought of personally and professionally. Over time, she develops a wide range of possible paths she is willing to explore. The coaching gave her the focus to move forward in her life.

Harper

Harper is concerned her daughter is struggling in school. All of a sudden, she's gone from a good student to a marginal student. Harper does not know what is changing until a parent-teacher conference, where the teacher describes her daughter's lack of attention, inability to sit still, and the struggle to focus. Harper is embarrassed—why was her daughter doing those things? The teacher suggests Harper have her daughter examined for possible Attention Deficit Hyperactivity Disorder (ADHD).

This explanation is news to Harper, but she has her daughter evaluated and learns about Executive Functioning Disorder within ADHD. This means her daughter struggles to plan and stay organized when completing a task. This explains why her daughter constantly misses assignment due dates and can't seem to find the materials she uses daily. Harper gains an understanding of her daughter's self-talk of being "stupid" or not confident academically, especially compared to her friends. Through research, Harper learns about strategies that can help, but feels like they are just scrambling and experimenting with possible solutions.

Chatting with Harper about these challenges, another mom suggests she look into an ADHD coach. This type of coach understands how an ADHD mind works, and can help children (and adults) develop strategies for challenging situations.

Harper finds a local coach specializing in student ADHD challenges. In the first meeting, the coach explains how an ADHD brain works differently (not negatively). With new strategies, her daughter finds out she can do all the things her friends do academically, once she knows more about how her own brain functions, how she should study, and the best tools to help plan.

Within three months of coaching, Harper's daughter raises her grades by one letter or more. Nights of significant homework assignments are no longer a trigger for dramatic, emotional meltdowns. Her daughter works on projects over the weekend without being prompted. Most importantly to Harper, her daughter builds the academic confidence she was lacking before.

Harper realizes that when faced with a challenge, you are more willing to take risks when you have the tools to be successful. From working with a coach, her daughter feels supported and appears stronger. Harper knows it is something that would have been very difficult for her daughter to achieve on her own.

Nadia

Since having kids, Nadia feels awful about how she looks. Some days it sneaks up on her. Mentally, she thinks she looks okay, then Nadia sees a picture of herself and feels like her brain has played a trick on her—her mental image does not match her physical appearance.

Nadia doesn't know why this continues to take her by surprise, but even worse, she is frightened by the severe self-talk she uses any time she is taken off guard by these images. She loathes her physical self in a way she doesn't feel about any other aspect of her life. Nadia doesn't know what is wrong with her, but the self-talk is draining and harmful.

Nadia's friend, a career coach, recently posted on social media about a health and wellness coach. Nadia has worked with various fitness coaches in her past and is not interested in returning to a gym. Yet when Nadia looks up the wellness coach online, she is surprised there is no mention of calorie counting or exercise repetition on the website.

Nadia reaches out online and completes a brief form. The coach sets up a free call to connect and see if it's a good fit. Since it is a phone call and not face-to-face, Nadia feels more confident opening up about what is bothering her. It is less about nutrition and exercise, and more about dealing with self-loathing. The only thing Nadia is sure of is that she wants it to stop.

Nadia and the coach agree to move forward through a three-month engagement by phone. It starts with Nadia reading a book and completing a workbook to process what she is learning. They discuss the workbook tasks on their calls, but more often than not, the workbook is just a prompt for deeper discussions. Nadia shares honest and personal observations about her own life and the world around her, including the constant messages of physical perfection. Her coach assigns Nadia mental rather than physical exercises—consciously shifting her self-talk. Sometimes these strategies feel goofy, but over time Nadia realizes the vicious, negative self-berating disappears.

After their coaching engagement, Nadia subscribes to her coach's monthly newsletter and social media updates. These act as quick reminders to stay on track based on the work she has accomplished. Nadia is relieved to have the days of negative self-talk behind her.

Takeaway

Progressing through life without the wisdom of others means experiencing just a sliver of what life can be. Learning and taking actions supported by coaches, then thriving with new thoughts and inspiration, can change and create a life larger than a dream.

What's one small step you can take today?

27

Transforming Dark-Cloud Days

The Challenge

I want to keep the lines of communication open with my children—especially when they are sad or depressed—but with our busy days, I may be missing out on opportunities to make that connection with my children on a deeper level.

Camryn's Story

Living with two girls, I know our emotional rhythms are somewhat in sync. The reality is there are times when we simultaneously feel sad. Each of us want to be alone and work through this emotion. It is like we can all be so connected and engaged, then suddenly "dark clouds" set in emotionally and we take a step away.

Depression and anxiety seem more common in our society and thread through so many lives. I worry my girls' tendency for strong emotions like depression may come from me. Although this is a normal emotion, it can separate us within our family and take time to examine or work through.

I want to help my girls recognize and address their feelings by using tools that shift them away from isolation and towards connection. It's not like I have mastered this myself, but I'm overwhelmed with guilt that they may suffer because of my natural tendencies, and I cannot fix it. What are some basic things I can do?

Taking Action

Emotions can be waves of energy we cannot process—especially when they are unexpected. It can be a beautiful, sunny day, and you plan to wake up filled with energy and grand aspirations. But something else settles in emotionally, you lose all motivation, and the day slips away. For both parents and children, this experience can be frustrating.

Depression can be a challenging topic for both children and parents to discuss. Developing safe, routine ways to express feelings can create habits and tools children will continue to use into adulthood. Seeking additional help may also be necessary.

Ways to Get Started

It is frequently reported that stress, depression, and anxiety are at an all-time high globally for children, teens, and adults. As a parent, managing your own emotional challenges combined with trying to monitor your child's struggles can be overwhelming. It may take experimentation with various strategies to find the right combinations that work for you or your child.

The most important part is communicating. Letting your child know you are struggling some days teaches them about dealing with depression at any age. In turn, creating specific times or practices where your child has the same space to feel safe and communicate with you is critical as they develop.

Camryn

At some point in college, when Camryn developed depression, she began creating a "toolkit" to lift her spirits—even just a bit—to make it through her days. As an adult, she realizes she still relies on that toolkit, and it serves her well.

Camryn knows that visual stimuli is helpful for her to reach her "happy place." She keeps a short video clip of some movie outtakes on her computer. While the film is not her absolute favorite, the outtakes—full of spontaneous, uncontrolled laughter—always lift her mood considerably in a matter of minutes. There is something contagious about watching others laugh without abandon. In addition, she keeps a series of clips in both her YouTube and TikTok accounts for quick pick-me-ups.

Camryn also keeps on her phone a digital picture of a child's art room full of paper, paints, chalks, and crayons. That image not only takes her back to a specific time and place in her childhood but also reminds her of a state of pure joy. She will close her eyes and mentally place herself there, trying to recognize, absorb, and even recreate all the sights, sounds, and sensory stimuli that remind her of the joyous feelings she had at that time.

Similarly, Camryn keeps a key song from her childhood on her phone. She played it so often as a teen, it is ingrained in her memory as a symbol of a simpler time. Now, when she struggles to fall asleep at night, singing the song in her head instantly relaxes her body. She has literally developed a soothing physical reaction to that piece of music. This combination of tools physically shifts her body, and in turn her mood when she recognizes she is feeling down and wanting to disengage.

Camryn is working to pass along this toolbox to her girls. When they are having a regular day, she asks them what their favorite memories are. They talk about their favorite movies, music, art, and events that relate to their personal feelings of joy, and Camryn takes note.

Now, when one of her daughters is struggling and sitting alone, Camryn senses when they are ready to talk and joins them. First, she brings up these favorites and asks them to sit with the feelings these uplifting items trigger. As it brings some emotional light into their day, Camryn feels she has created a safe space for them to communicate and share what is troubling them.

Jade

As her children move into their teenage years, Jade views their emotional stability as a roller coaster, not knowing how they feel moment to moment. She personally works to relate this back to her own teenage years.

Jade takes the time to remember how her emotions ran hot and cold as a teenager, how much she tried to be alone, and the times she felt like everything was the end of the world. In her childhood, Jade's parents didn't have the ability to help her through the low times, other than the traditional "pull yourself up" message. Now she wants to do better with her kids.

Jade is proud to have forged strong relationships with her children. With a little prodding, her kids usually open up about their struggles. Now, if they are particularly upset with an incident that felt like it was the "worst thing that could have ever happened," Jade uses a tool taught to her recently by her coach: the classic "Could it get worse?" trick, which trains the brain to think through the true level of negative possibilities, while putting the current one in perspective.

She walks her child through a scenario of, "Well, what could get worse after that?" It takes a few hypotheticals for her children to realize the current situation is not as dire as they thought and they are grateful the situation isn't any worse.

Jade is not trying to diminish their feelings. Instead, she wants them to learn to move challenges into the proper perspective so they are not personally overwhelmed. Occasionally, the conversation morphs to jokes of outlandish ways the situation could have been worse. Jade takes this as a sign her kids are learning to recognize their problems for what they are, and she doesn't want to diminish them, only help provide perspective.

After the "What could get worse?" exercise, Jade likes to flip the focus to "what if" with all positive outcomes. She sees her kids brighten as they investigate what productive actions they could take to turn these concerns around. This negative-to-positive path is a tool she believes will serve her children as they become adults.

Harper

Harper tries to respect her kids' boundaries and need for privacy when they head to their rooms to hang out. However, she worries about this isolation when she can tell they are feeling a bit down. Trying to talk to them can be challenging, as it feels like directly invading their space.

Harper has learned to take advantage of a safer space: the car. Running errands with one of her children allows them time alone. The distance from the separate seats in the vehicle also helps, because it facilitates personal conversation without forcing them into eye contact.

She knows sometimes it takes some prodding to get the conversation going with her children. Harper will first ask them to put away their device so they are fully engaged. As the conversation starts to flow, Harper deliberately takes the long way to their destination. Mentally, it can be challenging for Harper not to take the most efficient route or complete her errands promptly, as she has mentally conditioned herself. However, Harper knows this time and talk is precious. The to-do list will always be there.

Nadia

With her young children, Nadia gets frustrated her day is not her own. She never knows when the next tantrum will hit. Nadia feels driven to take advantage of quiet times—when the children are tired or settled—to create space for herself. She craves that personal time and can get cranky when her children demand it instead.

However, Nadia is starting to recognize her kids sometimes express their sadness by needing things like snuggle time. Nadia is used to creating those moments when her children go to bed at night. But depending on the day, her children may cling or ask to snuggle at times when Nadia is in the middle of something else. Nadia is realizing she needs to prioritize these moments and take the time necessary, regardless of what she was doing before.

Takeaway

Connecting with children includes creating spaces so they can communicate their needs or concerns. It also means recognizing and giving that time as a parent. It is so easy to say, "Wait until I'm done," before connecting. But these critical situations cannot wait. The effort and lessons that can be shared will outweigh other tasks and activities every time.

What's one small step you can take today?

28

SELF-CARE: Coloring for Creativity

The Challenge

Sometimes I feel the need to create and just let my artistic inner self out. But I have no talent nor experience, so how can I channel this desire without looking foolish?

Nadia's Story

Though daily routines keep me running, I'm finding I'm having trouble sitting still in the few minutes of downtime at the end of the day. I enjoy getting the kids through their bedtime escapades, but even after that, I'm restless. Sitting still in the evening seems like it would be restful, but my mind scrambles to think of the things I forgot to do.

Part of my restlessness is a nagging feeling I want to stretch myself creatively. Am I watching too many TikToks? I'm pretty sure I have no natural artistic talent—but I dabbled in art activities as a kid. Should I try again as an adult? Isn't this a thing now? I'm not sure what to try or how to even get started. I don't want to buy many supplies that turn into a pile of junk sitting around. What is a simple, no-brainer creative outlet?

Taking Action

Many people will claim they are not creative. However, coloring existing artwork is something we have been doing all our lives. As a kid, it was coloring books with crayons. Then in high school or college, the required art class had you branching into chalk, charcoal, pencils, or other mediums.

As an adult, you can finally move away from crayons and towards colored pencils, pens, or markers, using a smattering of "adult" coloring books. The sharpness of a pencil provides the opportunity to work on richly patterned designs called mandalas. There are also landscapes, animals, cities, and various other themes. In addition to books, it is easy to search online to find patterns to print.

Why coloring? Several observations:

- Coloring relaxes the brain and spirit and allows for a bit of daydreaming.

- Coloring while watching TV (mainly when kids watch the SAME movie for the hundredth time) keeps your hands busy (and not eating!).

- Coloring satisfies a creative need without sparking a substantial project or new hobby that might fade over time.

- Coloring tools (whether crayons or colored pencils) are not a significant cost investment.

- Coloring can bring a sense of creative balance, even just for an evening or an hour on the weekend. Kids will notice and sometimes take an interest in coloring with you.

If you thought adult coloring seemed silly or a fad, give it a try. Pick up a small set of colored pencils and a simple book that speaks to you. Sit in a spot with wonderful light and pick out a few colors that fit your current mood. Let your hands take over, and your mind wander. See what coloring can inspire in you.

Trying Another Medium

If you are looking for a bit of creativity with a higher jumping-off point, try adult paint-by-number. This is not the simplistic kit you used as a kid—six colors and a flat board. This artistic expression has also scaled to an adult pastime. Now you can order canvas-based works with complex variations of color and shadow worthy of concentration.

This activity allows you to fine-tune painting skills, but also lets your mind wander while creating. Your result may even be frame-worthy!

Need something more creative on the go? Try a paint-by-number phone app. Digital paint-by-number games can provide a wide assortment of image types, goals, and rewards based on what you color and how frequently you participate. In addition, in-application responses to touching the coloring spot (such as animated color fill) as well as haptic responses when you are finished with a color (a small vibration from your phone) can make the experience more interactive. Having this on your phone means you can do something more creative than a farming or candy-crushing game.

Wine and Painting

This is a fun evening with some girlfriends, often for charity. Everyone gathers at a location or painting studio where drinks are served, and a DIY paint company leads the class in creating a work of art. All materials are provided, and the instructor breaks down the approach to the painting, so you can see the elements and layers simplistically, but still bring your own style. Over time, you may accumulate several of these canvases, showing sunsets, forests, and more. It's like creating your own little art gallery at home.

Ways to Get Started

Whether completing something simple or starting to stretch yourself into new talents, bringing some tactile creativity into your life can help bring balance and peace.

Nadia

Nadia has a restlessness about creativity. She feels her mind, body, and spirit are craving some kind of creative outlet, but she has no idea what that could be. It is hard for her to consider that randomly doing something creative would be a good use of time.

Looking online one day, the idea strikes Nadia to make greeting cards. It is not difficult to find line art and other decorative items to print out. She also likes the idea of saying what she wants to say in a card. Most of all, Nadia figures cards are a simple way to color and get creative.

Nadia looks at her calendar for upcoming family birthdays. She scouts around for art that will be interesting to color and may have more meaning for the receiver than a generic card. Once she prints a few card outlines on some heavy paper, she purchases a set of colored pencils and gets to work.

She assembles a little carrying basket for the cards and pencils, so she can move it throughout the house. When the kids are down for a nap on the weekends, she allows herself to stop "catching up" on things and simply relax and color. Nadia finds listening to a podcast or documentary while coloring is the perfect mix for her brain to daydream. She is proud of the cards she creates and is excited to mail them to unsuspecting family members.

Takeaway

Creativity can take many forms. However, no one has to be the next great artist to kickstart their imagination. The simple act of bringing some guided creative process into your life can build a relaxing habit.

What's one small step you can take today?

Acknowledgements

The Challenge

I want to acknowledge every influence in my life, but I don't have enough pages.

I have a lifelong love of learning that keeps me buried in books. Having read many acknowledgments by many authors, I know it's challenging to recognize everyone who influences an author. These acknowledgements are my attempt to capture those people, and I apologize to anyone I have missed.

It is true writing is an isolated activity, and it is also mired with fits and starts. I have to thank Heather Doyle Fraser for keeping me motivated despite everything from quarantine to writer's block. Working with Heather has not only taught me so much about writing but about what actions I need to take in my life to be an inspired, creative individual. I am a better person for our time together.

My sister, Laura, was my first reader and critic. Those few souls who can tell you honestly how your thoughts resonate outside your head are rare. Despite my fear of sharing my writing, I knew my sister would simultaneously critique and support, and I cannot thank her enough.

My parents and brother helped shape who I am and how I approach my life. My dad, Jerry, instilled my work ethic while my brother, Chris, challenged my thoughts and expectations. Many of the book's examples and reflections are influenced by my childhood in which my mother, Karen, was a significant presence. Although I lost her to the complications from Alzheimer's earlier than anyone should, her spirit is woven through all of the women in this book.

My family both influences and inspires me. My daughter, Morgan, has helped me recognize how much I want to support her in being an even better person than I can be. She is also the artist who built subtle details of each personality into the icons that accompany them. In addition, my son, Ethan, teaches me empathy and compassion daily: traits that some days seem both mysterious and magical to me and ones I want to develop as completely as he does. Finally, my husband, Shawn, is a partner and supporter straight out of a novel. If I needed to step away from family life to write, he was there to pick up all the pieces and keep the family on track. He is my cheerleader who supports my ideas with a dose of logic, and I would never accomplish anything I try without his support. I can't ask for anything more.

Lastly, there are many friends who subjected themselves to the various assessments I've included to help frame the personalities of Camryn, Jade, Harper, and Nadia. Without their help, there would be no girlfriends to connect with. I am forever grateful they took the time to learn more about themselves, as well as inspire me.

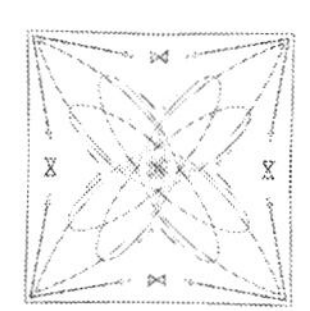

About the Author

Karrie Converse-Jones is a multi-passionate entrepreneur and founder of TurningLeaf Enterprises, LLC. which is an umbrella for her various creative and professional interests.

When not developing new ideas and businesses, Karrie enjoys traveling with her family around the world, reading on the beach, and finding any opportunity for either organizing or spa time.

Karrie lives in central Ohio with her husband, teenage daughter, and teenage son.

For more information about this book or Karrie's other entrepreneurial ventures, please visit:

www.girlfriendstoriesbook.com